MW01065933

Finding The Right Piece

Using Laughter and Faith in the Puzzle of Life

Jaime Rafferty

CROSS BOOKS

CrossBooks™
A Division of LifeWay
1663 Liberty Drive
Bloomington, IN 47403
www.crossbooks.com
Phone: 1-866-879-0502

First published by CrossBooks 4/2/2010

ISBN: 978-1-6150-7170-8 (sc)

Library of Congress Control Number: 2010924263

Printed in the United States of America
Bloomington, Indiana
This book is printed on acid-free paper.

DEDICATION

I now understand that without the saving grace of Jesus Christ I would have nothing. I'm thankful he has shown me how to love and let go of "who I was".

I thank my amazing husband Paul, who has loved me UNCONDITIONALLY. I am grateful that God gave us our precious children. Beau has allowed me to see the world in a different and captivating way. While Brynn's enthusiasm for life, inspires me to be a little more enthusiastic too! Paul, Beau and Brynn bring me so much joy and laughter, too much to keep to myself!

Though I am a work in progress I feel blessed to have been raised by MY Mom and Dad, and to have Matt as my "Big Brother". I am honored to be the granddaughter of Mammaw Evelyn and Pappaw Irnin, who are residing humbly in heaven! I know they are not missing us as they dance and sing on the streets of gold. I thank God they were our second parents.

Through some tough life circumstances, my amazing husband, family and friends have stood by me and supported me. I can't say thank you enough to my family and Paul's family for their love. I love you Marsha, Ed, Linda, Granny, Shannon, Bryan and Gaynelle (and the rest of the extended family)!

A very special thank you to my "book review" crew and to the MANY others who have supported and inspired me on this journey, laughed at my stories and continue to see God's glory in the funny little things of life!

Introduction

This is a glimpse into the heart of my husband, my son, my daughter, my parents, of course me and may even be a glimpse into your heart. I hope the stories you read will inspire you to laugh, a good belly laugh, or smile on a day when nothing seems to draw a smile from you. Or perhaps you will just lower your head, shake it side to side, as you read about the follies of the Rafferty family, and reflect on some of those moments in your own family that made you laugh. That would bless the Lord too; being thankful for your family and all the memories, you create together!

The stories are a GIFT from God, through the people he's placed in my life. I write this on faith, faith that someone will even want to read about an average flawed mom with a wonderful husband and two extraordinary children. Through this venture may He be glorified, and give us women the perseverance to work at being clothed in strength and dignity.

As I began to age, notice I didn't say mature, I had come to realize I wasn't a very good mother. Now your idea of being a good mother and mine could differ. I will tell you what I do well. I make sure they have clean clothes (though there may be a pile of dirty ones in the floor near the washer/dryer). I can make a mean chicken and cheese casserole that the whole family loves (you can never go wrong with crescent rolls). Paul and I take them to church every week. We take family trips together, whether it is around town or on a vacation. We play together, in the backyard, sometimes football, other times soccer and this year Paul is even threatening to set up a tent back there, pray for me! We especially love to snuggle. Our family may sound a lot like yours! Hey, I don't sound that bad, do I? Well, in the new age of motherhood, I think I have missed the mark! Why? I don't scrapbook, strike one! I'm not particularly good at photography, strike two! I'm really not good with scissors at all, just ask my high school home economics teacher, my childhood best friend and a few others who felt the pain of this left-handed art challenged freak. Crafts are particularly difficult for me, strike three! It looked like I was pretty much going to be a failure at motherhood, as a whole.

Until one day…something funny had happened at home the evening before, among the madness of raising two small children, one of which (Beau) didn't even like me half the time. I decided that instead of pouting about our circumstances with Beau or complaining about the mundane things of life, I could laugh and share the laughter with others. I had no idea if anyone would find them nearly as funny as I did but I didn't mind, I enjoyed writing them. We all have a story to tell. I decided to begin journaling the stories, forward them to my friends, family, and e-mail buddies. I was humbled by the response that these e-mails from our little family, had spurned. People thought this stuff was funny. I have always hated being laughed at, or feeling like I was the butt of a joke. This time they weren't laughing at me, but with me. Even if it was me that did something that warranted a laugh, I could laugh about it too. That felt great. I was like Sally Field at the Academy Awards, I'm paraphrasing here: "They like me, they really like me!" It kind of felt like I had been accepted by my peers, of course minus the accolades and offers of film roles!

The last ten years of my life haven't been perfect, I have been far from perfect, but by God's grace and mercy, I invite you along for the ride for what I have found to be some of the highlights of our lives. So follow me; and my family as we live a crazy life and laugh at things you may or may not find funny. If this book does nothing for you other than help you to "laugh at the days to come", God has done a work that needed to be done in you and continues to do the same for me. Or maybe some of the reflections I have on life, scripture and whatever else I may say may also be things that you can relate to. Are you ready? Let's go!

I'd Need a Savior

I live a blessed life, really beyond anything I deserve. I want to share these blessings through letting you peek into the life of my family. For years, like so many people, I tried to find peace in places true peace, will probably never be found. Have you been there too? You know down roads that God didn't want you to travel? This may be through the acquisition of material possessions (to get a credit card bill that makes you cringe), taking on roles not designed for us (I'm the woman what was I thinking?), selfish acts (there is no I in team!), and the laundry list could just go on; it's that material and worldly stuff that looks so shiny and pretty at first, but then just leaves you empty. Though "empty" in my quest for "happiness", I had plenty of "stuff" and baggage to carry around after the road dead ends. I think we all can relate to this. However, God through his saving grace is helping me everyday find the right piece that was missing. We can all find plenty of things to try to find happiness in our lives. He reminds me there is only one piece that fits, Jesus.

It's a battle as old as Adam and Eve, human (my) will vs. God's will. We know how that story went, with Adam and Eve right. Getting kicked out of the Garden of Eden, evicted really. These two had it made in paradise! Sometimes as I have read this story, I am hoping for a different ending. "Come on Eve, don't do it…don't do it". Or I may be thinking, "Man up, Adam, this is your time to show her who's the head of this household", always to have the same outcome. They eat the forbidden fruit. We are no different in that we must try it "our" way, over and over again, when we know the outcome too! The result is usually a dead end some where between misery and spiritual famine. When I end up there, I think, "How did I get here?" I know how I go there; it usually doesn't make me feel any better though! We are human and though given the foresight, we still think we can "outsmart" divine wisdom, only to fail. Gosh, we must love to learn things the hard way! I love the phrase, "if you do what you've always done, you will get what you've always gotten". Isn't that a fitting analogy for how we often live our lives? Thankfully, God knew we needed a Savior, a man in skin, the ONLY man, Jesus. He came to help show His mercy, grace and love. To be the ultimate sacrifice because man will always eat of the proverbial forbidden fruit.

Man, has a hard time letting go of the past, but God says, once we confess our sins and turn from them they are cast "as far as the East if from the West". Sometimes we are the ones who have the problem, letting go. I don't know about you, but I often will pick things up, carry them around and be burdened as if I have never asked God to help me move forward. Then I whine about having a back ache. Something that I am learning everyday through God's grace is that I have to check the "baggage" at the throne and start living and enjoying the gifts, I have here on Earth. But, I should use those lessons learned as building blocks of faith, teachable moments from the Father.

Like many of you, I wear a lot of hats. I am a wife, mother, daughter, granddaughter and friend. However, there is another hat that sits at the top of my closet, just waiting to be worn, that's the sinner hat. Oh it looks like it would go with any outfit, that's what's so tricky about it. I am learning to use the tools God has given, through his instruction book, the bible, to keep that hat in a place where it isn't staring me right in the face. From observations of his teachings it seems that God doesn't want us to dwell on the "sinner", but moreover realize we are sinners and that's why we need him. Dwelling on being the sinners that we are can get in the way of doing the work He has called us to do.

Though being a sinner is a given for all of us, I am really glad it's not a requirement it on my resume. That would be impressive, huh? When you think about it, sinner doesn't quite have the majestic ring or roll off the tongue like "Mother", "Child of God" or all of the other roles we have assumed or are assigned. Ooh SINNER, not so much a noteworthy title. Sometimes I even wondered if I am qualified for any of those other roles, and no, I guess I'm not. We are lucky that He fulfills them in us, each of those roles, if we allow him and give him reign in our lives. Trust me, you will see just how faulty I am and I won't be dwelling on all mistakes, or this book would be a novel.

As I began to hear God correct my path, my heart seemed drawn to Proverbs 31. From there I wanted to be more like her, then, I wanted learn more about her. In my reading, I came upon something that spoke VOLUMES to me. Proverbs 31:25 – "She is clothed with strength and dignity; she can laugh at the days to come." Reading that gave me a glimpse into the woman I would like to be. What sealed the deal for me was to see that she can laugh at the days to come…yee-haw! There it is…laughter. I love it! Imagine that, God wanting us, His greatest creation, to enjoy His other creations. This Proverbs 31 woman has the formula! Outside of her ability to laugh, which is a recurring theme here with me, I was much more impressed that she was clothed with strength and dignity. I would venture to guess this is why the laughter comes easier. I never thought of my wardrobe consisting of strength and dignity, but now I am viewing it as an essential piece of my attire and if it's from God's closet, I bet everyone would wear it well.

I really enjoy "God" time and being alone with him. It's just me, getting to know myself, through studying His word, just being still in his presence. Or not being so "still", my Mammaw Evelyn used to tell me that because I couldn't sit still I had the Saint Vitas Dance, it's a true disorder, look that one up. She thought that I was where the phrase, "Have you got ants in your pants" came from. I am still like that, just "antsy". However, I have learned how to ask God to help me be still, in my mind and my spirit.

Sometimes when I'm being still in His presence, I may be me behind the wheel of my car, driving to work after I have dropped the kids off at school. It doesn't have to be kneeling beside your bed, though that's a great place too. I am allowing Him to reign in me at that moment. I may not verbally be still. Sometimes I am praising Him at the top of my lungs to my favorite Christian songs as drive down a busy street. I am sure, though this isn't the prettiest sight, should you pass me, bopping my head and moving side to side; he appreciates all the praise I can give him. He is worthy of our praise. And by the way, should you witness my time with God in the car, don't judge me, I bet you do it too and look great while you're at it!

I absolutely love people! Sometimes to husband's (Paul) dismay, like when I run into a store for a quick errand and then I see five people I just couldn't go without saying hello too, or giving a hug. God has given me the ability to relate to people, to make people laugh. Well, not all people laugh, but some people. I have to say I did want another gift, which you will hear about later. But, I will embrace the one God has given me. In today's topsy-turvy and negative world, laughter is a much needed past time. I know even this very day; I could use a little more laughter. I do not know what is going on in your life, BUT I would almost guarantee you could use a laugh too. I am going to assume if you could not use a laugh or need a bit of inspiration that you would not have picked up this book. I sure hope it's a good book or you're going to be pretty disappointed with your selection, my friend. Right now, together, let's choose to believe this book is going to be good! Whew, at least I feel better.

Beauty is Fleeting

I'm not sure there is any true "order" to our stories. Does life really have that much "order" anyway? If you say yes, I would have to challenge your answer, because I know for me personally the more prepared we try to be the more chaotic our life seems to become. According to scripture, "I (God) know the plans I have for you". Often times the two don't coincide…our plan and His plan. From here on out, I gotta go with His plan. Mine has been a royal mess!

So instead of starting at the beginning, which according to Julie Andrews in the Sound of Music is a very good place to start, how about I start….here and now? ☺

Continuing on our Proverbs 31 theme with the next verse to illustrate a story read with me:

Proverbs 31:30 (New International Version)

[30] Charm is deceptive, and beauty is fleeting; but a woman who fears the LORD is to be praised.

Some translations of the Bible will use the word vain or vanity instead of beauty. I fight vanity probably every day of my life.

This is what I affectionately refer to as Retainer Gate. I have this (vain) obsession with my teeth. It's almost scary... really. I dream they get knocked out, I lose them in some freak accident, all kinds of weird mishaps involving my teeth. I think this is because when I was a teen my parents graciously put braces on my teeth. I say graciously because I did not feel braces were a rite of passage. I knew that our financial situation wasn't great at the time, however they did it anyway. My teeth were straight; they just had gaps in the front of them. My Dad used to say loving things like, "Jaime, you could eat a pumpkin through a slat fence". You can see how he was a pillar in building my self-esteem as a kid.

I got my braces off in January of 1995, and to this day, I still wear my original retainer, it's because of these strange fears (and vanity!), and a shifty side tooth. Paul finds this absolutely hysterical, that his wife wears a retainer to bed at a minimum of 350 evenings a year (probably more!). One night I was lying in bed, and a back piece broke of this ancient retainer. I almost cried, seriously just about lost it. Some might think these teeth are my pride and joy, no, not even close, okay so maybe close.

I thought I noticed the next morning that without this one little piece, that I almost swallowed, the shifty side tooth seemed miles away from my big front tooth. I had to call the old orthodontist's office. I thought the lady was going to laugh me off the phone. I told her how long I had the retainers and that I really appreciated all the money my Mom and Dad spent on making my teeth nice. She said, "Honey we LOVE patients like you!" through her laughter. She then told me that she had to go upstairs and DIG through the files to see what course of action we needed to take.

I was keeping my fingers crossed for an easy find in the "chart dig". I almost offered to come up there and help her to expedite the process but I had work of my own to do. Luckily, I got a return phone call from the office and with an "A-ha" tone she tells me the file has been located and we make the appointment.

I walked in and the office looked just as I remember it... circa 1995. However there is a new "check-in" system and my old brain had trouble navigating it. Apparently whoever I spoke to on the phone that day told everyone in the office about the "old lady" who still wore her retainers. I was the "dog and pony show" for the morning.

Benita (who I remember from back in the day) welcomed me back to a consultation room and told me that I hadn't changed a bit. Benita might want to consider having her eyes examined. Surely I didn't look like THAT kid anymore. Anyway she evaluated my retainers and said they were in great shape (thank you, thank you very much!). She seated me as she autoclaved the disgusting 15 year-old retainers. I waited for the doctor. When she came back she told me she had some photos of me. I suppose I wanted to torture myself and asked to see them. Mind you, these are the photos she refererenced when saying I hadn't changed a bit. They were on a microfilm (I felt SO old). The date on the photo said June 1992. I held the pictures up to the light and just about FELL OUT OF THE CHAIR. Why my mother let me look like that and didn't tell me was a crime against humanity. I laughed so loudly I almost busted a gut! My teeth were, well they were a lot different than they do now, and I bet I could have driven a Cadillac through them. I looked like I was the mold for the infamous "Billy Bob Teeth" that were popular years ago, here and around the South. The frames of my glasses were as big as soft balls and my hair looked like birds were nesting in it. I kept aqua net and white rain in business apparently during that time. That girl looked so unassuming.

As I am trying to compose myself from laughter the orthodontist makes his entrance. The retainers fit "beautifully" according to the doctor. They tightened them and they felt like a MILLION BUCKS! The staff seemed thrilled at the state of my teeth. He told me I didn't have to wear them every night...I told him because he had those photos around I would ALWAYS wear the retainer...he jokingly said, "They are a part of you aren't they", DUH, it's 15 years later and I am sitting in YOUR office, it's not rocket science, YES they are a part of me. I take better care of my teeth and retainers than most things other things I own, kids included!

I get to the front desk to check out and they tell me, "I am family" and don't charge me a cent! I felt like I was in the mafia and it felt GREAT! So "suckas" who's laughing now?

I have to remind myself that if my teeth ever happen to "shift" back to my pre-braces days or they fall or get knocked out, it's not the end of the world. Beauty, by the world's standard is fleeting! We live in a time where we try to constantly "fix" beauty. I'm now inclined to laugh at these foolish fears about my teeth, and though I will continue to take care of them, I need to be spiritually working on the "rest of me"!

Gift of Gab?

Is it already obvious that I am undeniably silly? If not, one of my favorite things to do is to try to make Paul laugh, especially if he has had a hard day at work. I will go into the living room and do my best at least to get him to crack a smile, but I would rather see an all out laugh. In my routine of getting him to laugh, I will make faces or do a little funny strut/walk. However, the highlight of the little charade to try to make him laugh is to dance. Now, I don't mean just any dance, but a 1990's favorite…the Running Man, and if I am feeling especially goofy, I might even pull out a Cabbage Patch, and I am not talking about the doll…but the dance, just for good measure. Some of you may be reading this racking your brain wondering what a Running Man or a Cabbage Patch is. Before you wonder any further, much like me singing in the car with no one but me and God in there, these dances aren't pretty, at least when I performing them. But, I'm having a good time and giving it my all. Another favorite Rafferty past time that I think I get from my Dad, is take a song and change the words to fit your circumstance. This is usually a family montage, Paul, me, and both kids. Nine times out of ten, we butcher a perfectly good song to interject our bad or funny circumstance just to muster a laugh. It's good times!

Some people affectionately (others without so much affection) tell me that God has blessed me with the gift of gab. Yes, this is sometimes a blessing, and other times a curse. I am not proud to tell you this, but I could literally talk to a tree, I don't need interaction. I also have "one of those voices".

My office is in a multi-level building. The floor that I am on has open hallways. If someone that knows me is coming up the staircase and I am talking, without fail they will say aloud, "Jaime, I knew I heard your voice". Oh great, I always think, I'm such a loud mouth. I often hear from different people that my speaking voice is unique. I don't necessarily think it's a compliment and hope it's not a fingernails scraping on the chalkboard type of sound. It's kind of embarrassing, but what can you do?

When in college I actually took a class called Voice and Diction. I loved it. Something about that class was a bit ironic. The professor was from Minnesota and was trying to teach a bunch of kids (the majority of us) from Western Kentucky how to enunciate properly. All the while, she had this precious, Swedish accent to her voice. I always say, "Yeah, sure ya betcha, the coooooookies are in the oven". That's how Dr. Payne sounded to me. However, I am sure my western Kentucky peers and I sounded like we hadn't left the hills and hollers of the Bluegrass State and we needed her "coaching".

Even more embarrassing than being extremely talkative is I think I am a pretty entertaining person. Pitiful, right? Maybe I have just lowered my entertainment standard. You know, that I find myself funny. Let me rephrase that before I sound like I could use a trip to the "Humble Bakery" and get a whole humble pie for myself. I guess what I really mean to say is the older I get, the less entertainment I need from others. Yeah, that's what I meant to say, it's not that I am just so hysterical, it's that I have begun to appreciate the funny little things that happen. I am not talking about standing up in front of a crowd trying to make them laugh, per say (though I would think that was fun too), I mean it's okay for me to be by myself and laugh at myself whether I am trying to be funny or life hands me a funny. I had no choice to but to grow up and be this way.

The Bionic Woman? Not so Much!

I come from very humble beginnings. I was born to working class parents in a small town in Kentucky. I would have to say I think it is a town with character and nothing reflects that more than the town motto. As you arrive in the city limits, you are welcomed by a sign that reads: "Home of 2000 Happy People and a Few Soreheads". When I've been asked, which one I was, I would often say depended on which day of the week you asked if I was one the happy ones or I was in the handful of soreheads. From my experience of living in this town, I met many more happy people than I did soreheads.

Things were somewhat comical for me, and my family from the start. Case and point…one year Mom and Dad welcomed a beautiful baby boy, Matt come on a lovely September day. Three short years later, the sweet family of Father, Mother and Son welcomed a beautiful baby girl, Jaime on that very same date in September. You guessed it, that's me! I was stealing Matt's thunder from my first day on earth, being born on his special day and all. I think I was a point of contention for Matt from the very first day of my little life. I am sure I was the last thing he wanted for his birthday. I personally could think of far worse presents than me, but for a three year old, I am sure I didn't even make his wish list.

It has been said that I was to be named Leslie Brianne but apparently, I didn't look as much like a Leslie as my parents would have hoped. So instead, they made the next logical choice, which was to name me after a 70's icon, Jaime Somers, The Bionic Woman. Talk about a tall order. How was I ever supposed to live up to that? My parents had no idea how much pressure this put on me. Yeah right, it was probably 1994 before I had even heard of the show. But, I never saved anyone, I was never a good runner, basically a let down to the name, however being bionic couldn't be all it's cracked up to be. I bet it was like being an expensive car, you know your body parts were probably pretty hard to come by!

One irony I have appreciated since grade school was that I befriended another Jaime. Apparently the first day we met we both had on shirts that sported our unique spelling on the back with velour lettering. I suppose we were fashion forward wanting all the other first graders to know our names from the start. I was the more "bold" of the two of us. I have always been more outspoken, while she is the demure dark haired beauty. However, she balanced me out…she still balances me out, and also wears her retainer every night, thank you very much!

We have been known to arrive at functions wearing the same dress. So not only did we have the same name we also have/had similar fashion choices. In addition we have been asked if we are sisters or related in some manner. Perhaps what they say is true, the more time you spend with someone the more you begin to look alike. I just hope I inherit her sweet spirit.

Through out school we were often seen together or were placed in the same classes. This often posed a problem, having the same name and all, so a solution was created. She would be known as Jaime H. and I would be known as Jaime D. When we would put our names on our papers, I don't know about her, but I would often put Jaime D. because that became part of my identity. To this day when people ask me about her, they don't say her last name, they will say, "How is Jaime H. doing?" I get tickled thinking of us as "thirty-somethings" and people still trying to remember who's who between us. We have a friend, Andi, who will often calls her "H." for short. I wonder if she has ever called me "D."?

Some of my youngest memories were of my brother and me in our "first" home. I remember our pets, our neighbors, our first swing set. The house had exchange vents in the floor; to this very day, I fear those vents. My young mind ran rampant at the thought of what lie below those pesky vents. I hope I never find out! Most of the reflections of my first childhood home are beautiful and sweet memories. One of my first incidents later became a staple in the family arsenal of stories. It took place when I was about three.

My Dad is an avid lover of cars, trucks and motorcycles. This very day he owns five vehicles. We have recently joked, one more car, truck or whatever and he will have to get a used car license just to park them at the house. I don't ever remember hearing my Mom make a fuss about any of his vehicular hobbies. He even owned a few motorcycles in his day. At the ripe old age of three, he was letting me ride passenger on one his bikes. As I think of that right now, I am nauseous. My own baby girl is seven and I wouldn't want her on a motorcycle now for anything. On this particular occasion, Dad got his way and we rode to my Mammaw and Pappaw's house. Now, I'm not sure exactly how far it was from our house to theirs but I will approximate about 6-7 miles. The trip there was without incident. The trip home was without incident too, pretty much. The only thing that happened was that the big monstrous helmet got turned all the way around. Meaning I was probably only seeing the black lining of the big ole' helmet, as opposed to the beautiful sunlight of the day. When my parents see this and remove the helmet, word on the street is they said, "Why didn't tell that your helmet was turned backwards?" to which I responded, "I just didn't want to bother anyone". What a precious child! I must have been a JOY to parent at that time. Apparently that was the last time I was ever so meek and gentile. I learned to complain with the best of them later in toddler hood.

I remember being quite gullible as a kid. If my Dad said it, I believed it. Dad was, and still is a jokester. He really enjoyed picking on my brother and me. This irritated my Mother beyond words. However, she knew it was a losing battle to fight over it, so she just let it be. Now, I am not saying I always liked it, but I think I am a little (with the emphasis on little) more resilient for it.

The gullibility set in when I was young, very young. I can't recall the exact age but that is a trait that never left me. Probably one of the funniest things I can recall was my Dad, saying he had an identical twin brother Jerry. Now, one might think this is the obvious right? Not me! Uncle Jerry was so much nicer than his identical twin brother, Dad. When he came to the house, he would never stay long and I never saw him and Dad in the same room, together. It also should have been a red flag when Mammaw had never even heard of this elusive twin Jerry, and she carried Dad in her womb for nine months. But, I was convinced he existed and was more than just an alter ego. But as Matt and I got older, Uncle Jerry came around, less and less. I still miss that guy!

When I was around four we moved, approximately a mile or so from the first home I lived in. My parents still reside in this house. It's a nice neighborhood. Because I'm from a part of what is labeled "rural" Kentucky (I would estimate about 90% of Kentucky falls into this category), I would meet people and they would ask me if I lived on a farm, or out in the country. I would almost laugh because we had houses across the street from us, on both sides of us, and after a few years, even houses were built behind my parents' home. It was a neighborhood. So to answer that question, "NO", I never lived on the farm, or what I would deem as the country.

Now, before I come away from this sounding all worldly, let me tell you about the road you must travel to get back to the neighborhood in question. It was a very narrow two-lane road. In some areas if you weren't hugging your side of the road, it was possible you could hit an oncoming car. To make matters a little more dangerous, there was only one way into the neighborhood and one way out. In addition, as time passed there were also animals grazing on either side of the narrow road. Are you convinced yet that I didn't grow up in the country? I have been corrected by my friend Lisa, she has told me to "face it", and I am from the "country". I will never agree to that.

I have to say the worst part of living in this neighborhood, for me, came in 1996. I worked at a local grocery store; I was a cashier, going to college full-time. That winter, we had a heavy snowfall. I remember school was cancelled, and I thought I was home free from responsibility that week. I couldn't have been more wrong. The owner of the store, just so happened to live in the neighborhood AND he owned a 4-wheel drive SUV. Imagine my surprise when I personally get a call from him asking if I would work. He would provide me transportation to and from the store. Oh how lucky! He was such a wonderful person to work for, it was impossible for me to say, "no". However, that was the longest week of my teenage life.

This neighborhood me and the grocery story owner lived in, had somewhat of a "reputation". There were some people were under the assumption that if you lived in this neighborhood, you must be wealthy. Apparently, I missed the memo on that one, as did my parents. I think anyone who has a 1986 baby blue Chevette, as I did, as my first vehicle in 1995. You are not from money. And, if you are from money, you must hide it very, very well. This car of mine, picture it if you will, a 4-door dull baby blue Easter egg. I had a pet name for this car; it was the "Shovette", because I wanted nothing more than to shove it off a cliff to its death. That never happened and I am ashamed I felt that way about it. You know, I'm not even sure the car was a four cylinder. I often felt I could do better I could just "Fred Flintsone" it. You know, tear the floorboards out and just use my feet. It had absolutely NO power. This car carried several misadventures but there are a couple that stand out more vividly.

One evening I was driving my precious little pastel egg through "town" with a carload of my girlfriends. I believe there were five of us in the car. I was in an area where the speed limit was 45. One of the girls says, "Hey Jaime, floor it". My friend Lisa (remember she's the one that reminds me how country I am) yells back, "What are you talking about, it is floored". She was right; I was lying on the gas and going 35, at best. In that car's defense, it ran until it had well over 250,000 miles on it. I guess I should say it jogged, I don't think that car ever made it up to a run!

On a separate occasion, my friend Jill and I were driving down main street minding our own business. As we were singing along to the music, we heard and felt the little car backfire. As if my life was so hard at that age, I remember thinking "GREAT". It's not like I loved this car as some people relish their first vehicles. It was more the thought of being without a car that was much worse. My thoughts then shifted to the prospect of the car being on its last leg and me having to get a new used car. I liked that thought much more than being car-less. That thought, wasn't so bad! I really should have been thinking more about the car being able to get somewhere to have it looked at before everyone on the street thought a gunfight was breaking out.

Luckily, my friend and I were very close to the service station that repaired our family cars. I drive into the lot, and exit the go-kart with a motor. As I walk up to the mechanic, I can feel my heart still in my throat. That feeling hit me at the sound of the loud "boom" that had filled the midday air. I debriefed the mechanic on what had occurred just moments before my arrival to his shop. He nodded reassuringly and said he wanted to drive it around the block for himself. That was a great idea. I hoped the car would cooperate and recreate the scene while he was driving so he could experience the horror firsthand. He hops in, drives away and is gone for about 3 minutes. My friend and I stand there over dramatizing the moment and discuss how scary it was when it happened. He pulls back in to the station lot. I am standing there awaiting his reaction to the situation and to my surprise; he is smiling from behind the wheel. I am not sure if this is a good thing, or a bad thing. He steps out of the car, approaches me and says, "Can I ask you a question?" "Yeah", I say. He continued by asking if we had seen a little white pick-up truck anywhere in our vicinity. Now this truck was known about town. It was owned by a couple of brothers that I knew pretty well. I said, "Yeah, they were about 2 cars in front of us, why?" He then begins laughing uncontrollably, "Jaime, that was THEIR truck backfiring, not your car". I don't say anything; all that comes out is "Really". I'm deflated inside. Not quite sure if it was, happiness that I wouldn't be without a car, humiliation because I can't even tell if my own car is backfiring, or just relief that that moment was over and I could walk away.

My friend and I very quietly re-enter the little blue car you could have heard a pin drop. We sit there for a minute in silence. Almost in disbelief, it wasn't my car. I shake my head in embarrassment. Sweet Jill then says, "Jaime, I don't know if this makes you feel any better or not, but I thought it was your car too". But for some reason, I didn't feel better at all, however I am grateful to have had a "Pollyanna" friend. Before my junior year of college, my Mom and Dad did surprise me with another car. It was also blue but was much sportier than the "Shovette". I would be remiss to complain too much about my first car. As that lovely second piece of metal I was the proud owner of, encountered as many problems, if not more, than the Chevette. My Dad once joked that the second car had a 100,000-mile guarantee. He later told me, "You can guarantee after 100,000 on that car, you will need a new motor". He was right, just as the mileage rolled over to 100,000 the engine blew. Dad is such a wise sage.

It's funny, well it's not really, but I will laugh anyway, I have terrible "luck" with cars. I think it's because I have been afraid of cars and driving since I was a kid. I have always contributed this fear to my Mammaw. She never obtained a driver's license. I was told that when she was a young lady, her brother let her drive his car and she had a little accident in it. I am not sure the extent of the damage, or if there really was any by today's standards, but regardless, that impacted her and kept her from ever driving. Hearing this story throughout my youth, I had sort of taken her fear onto myself. She never told me to be scared, I just was. I didn't get my driver's license until I was about a month shy of turning 18. I always had a fear of wrecks, and with that I also had driving anxiety. My stomach would knot up before I had to go anywhere, I would feel sick. This was something I often said I gave to the Lord, but always held onto it.

I had a few mishaps behind the wheel as a "young driver", but all were minor, very minor. With that, you would think I really would not have driving anxiety because I didn't really ever see anything I should be too afraid of. It was not until a couple of years ago that I had myself a pretty good wreck. That summer Paul and I were able to buy a new car, I thought it was beautiful and I loved the car, really loved it. At the point of the accident, I had the vehicle for four weeks. I had my daughter with me, who was four at the time; it was a HOT August day. We had just left the YMCA to go school supply shopping at Wal-Mart for my son, who was about to begin kindergarten.

We were driving south and I notice a teenager sitting in a turning lane and she just kept creeping out to turn, but I had the right of way to continue straight. As I am approaching the intersection where she is attempting to turn, I had to time to realize, we were about to hit one another. I collided with her as she turned in front of me. I had never had a wreck like that, an impact like that. BAM!

After impact, I really thought I was dead. Though I am being serious, I often laugh, because I opened my eyes saw the dust from the air bag and thought, "am I in Heaven"... then as I regained my wits about me, I was like, "If yes, then the Streets of Gold look just like the street I was driving on before I wrecked...I really did live in Heaven on Earth". As I realized God had not called me home to glory the pain set in. I remembered my daughter was in the car. I began screaming her name and asking her if, she was okay. I hear her start to sob and say, "Mommy, why did you wreck our new car". All I could do at that point was cry even more. I joke now that I said, "Because I wanted too". No, poor thing, she had daylights scared out of her too.

We walked away from that wreck with minor injuries. She had a black eye and I had pretty good case of whiplash, a busted lip, air bag burns and bruising. Overall, we looked great. I joke that burns on my hands did look like a flesh-eating virus for a few days, which was fun!

After that, I was told about something funny I did as the police were asking me questions. I kept saying repeatedly that I had only had the car for four weeks, I suppose I was trying to garner sympathy, like that was going to fix the car. The officer asked me about towing the car. I give him a name (who knows what I said; I think I was in shock). About a month or two after the accident, a friend of mine sees me and says, "How are you doing, since your wreck?" I asked her how she knew I had a wreck. Her husband sold us the car and apparently, under my duress I gave his name to tow my car. Think about it, imagine his surprise when he received a phone call saying, "A Mrs. Rafferty has been in a wreck and has given us your name to tow her car". I was so embarrassed. I am sure he thought he was through with us after the sale, and there I go giving him work to do. He had impeccable service after the sale though, he took care of everything, even had it towed to the car lot where we had made the purchase. Bet he did not realize I thought he ran a wrecker service too! So if you are in town and need to buy a car, call my friend Lydia's husband, I cannot promise you he will give you that special service if you wreck, but he is a great person!

We were able to purchase another new car after that. Actually the day of purchase of the other new car, I could only drive it around the parking lot because I had been on pain medication for at least a week. Paul is asking me how

I think it drives. I literally felt like I was backing it out of my garage, and then pulling it back in, I didn't really drive it at all, but it was sharp! I was so leery driving it after that ordeal but the driving anxiety did subside, a bit (can you believe that?). Then…it happened again. I was leaving a meeting to return to my office for an afternoon conference call with my bosses and colleagues. It was a cold and rainy February afternoon. I was only about 3 – 4 miles from my office when proceeding through an intersection with a green light I see out of my peripheral vision a car coming at me. Thankfully, the car hit my rear driver fender but spun me 180 degrees through an intersection. I am praying I do not hit another car or a utility while trying to maintain control of the wheel. My car comes to a complete stop, void of any cars, utility poles or anything else. A nice man who had witnessed the entire accident stayed with me until the police arrived. He came up to my window and I sit there crying until the police arrived. He said, "Ma'am I know you have just been in a wreck, but I promise you it could have been worse". I nodded, and said, "I know and thank you". He said, "No, really, I mean it, I have only seen driving like that in NASCAR, you had such control". I laugh about that now and am very thankful it wasn't worse. I knew the back end of my car was pretty beat up. But, I could not get out of the car. I could not look at it. I felt like a baby, but I just did not want to see it until the police and Paul got there.

I did finally have to look at it. It was still drivable but the rear bumper and part of the fender looked like it was going to scrape the ground, as it hung on ever so slightly. Paul and I called my Dad, who worked a couple of blocks from the accident, to come and drive my car to the body shop for me. I was too shaken up to drive.

We follow him to the repair center. He gets out of my car and we get out of Paul's car. All three of us are standing there with our hands on our hips until we are able to get an estimate. Its silence, until Dad says something along the lines of, "Well I know it won't make you feel any better, but even with the bumper almost dragging the ground, that thing drives well". At least his observation was good for a laugh.

Up to this point, I have yet to wreck again. I remain the butt of many jokes among friends and family members. People are obviously afraid to ride with me; though I often point out, I was not the one at fault in either wreck. They then tell me that I should drive a car advertising Target stores. Cause it's like when I am driving, I am a moving target, go ahead…laugh…it will do you good. However, my daughter did share some of her insight with my in-laws and I am more inclined to agree with her theories.

After church, one Sunday Brynna was riding with her grandparents to a Mexican Restaurant to meet Paul, Beau and I along with some other family members for lunch. She says to them, "Why do people always hit my Mom's cars?" She proceeds to say, "She gets hit from the front, she gets hit from the back". My in-laws say, "We don't really know honey". Brynn then gives the most logical answer I think I have heard, she says, "Maybe the people are just driving around with patches covering both eyes". Well Brynn that HAS to be the reason, because there really is no other logical explanation!

Our Mouths Were Filled with Laughter

I know I have joked about my neighborhood, my cars, my driving abilities, or lack there of, and my family. I will continue to do so through out this journey called life however, my parents and grandparents did instill in my brother and I to be thankful, regardless of your circumstances. I learn this the hard way, every day. It is for that reason I am supposed to share, with people some of the blessings, lessons and struggles we have seen along the way.

Apart from this girly-girl exterior of make-up, hair and costume jewelry, I am much deeper than the surface might reveal. I really am. I think a lot. I sit around and think... about conversations I have been apart of, issues of the world, scripture, actions (my own and others), epiphanies that the Lord has given me through bible study. Sometimes when I am in the car, as a passenger, I just look up at the clouds and start pondering all of God's creation. Talk about magnificent! I mean I try to process everything. Sometimes my mind feels like a circuit that is on overload with too many items plugged into one outlet. Unfortunately, my thinking often blurs into worrying. Apart from giving me the greatest gift of all in Jesus, he has also given me a good solution to help with my worry, and that is journaling. Writing is one of my ways of casting my cares upon the Lord. Sometimes I write down prayers in the journal, sometimes I feel like I am just conversing with God as I'm journaling. It's a release that helps me to reflect and move through certain situations with God's help. I haven't mastered the art of not worrying yet, and I may never, but I'm happy God has given me a tool to work through the worry.

Please read, Psalm 126 and then re-read it again, that's an order! Oh, did I mention, I'm a little bossy too, just like my Mom! She's bossy in a "get things done way", I'm bossy in a "I think this is a good idea" way. As you continue reading you will see that I probably would get a lot more accomplished if I had my Mom's kind of bossy. Oops, back to the scripture. See there I go, not getting things done again,

Now, I am going to somewhat dissect this scripture. I hope you will bear with me on this one. I am, in NO WAY, a bible scholar, nor do I play one on television. I am a person, just like you, reading through the magnificent word of God. All the way, I'm learning how to be the best Christian Wife, Mother, Friend, Daughter…whatever God wants me to be, I am going to aim for it.

In this specific passage, I am struck by what the author relays to the reader.

(Psalm 126:2)

"Our mouths were filled with laughter, our tongues with songs of joy. Then it was said among the nations, The LORD has done great things for them."

Did you see that? I knew I liked God! "Our mouths were filled with laughter". Now that is some good stuff, at least I think so, cause I love to laugh! I know for me, this is a hard pill to swallow sometimes. We as Christians must never forget what God has delivered us from (our captivity) and how he continues to deliver us daily, if that doesn't make you smile, laugh and jump up and click you're heels then I don't know what to tell you. However, I have a hard to, thinking how he could love someone like me, so faulty and unappreciative.

In many Old Testament passages, people were often captive to a geographical region where they experienced both spiritual and physical hardships/captivity/slavery. In our lives, God has often delivered us from spiritually desolate places. We don't have to live in that desolation for the rest of our lives. No matter what held us captive! We are the ones who often hold ourselves captive by filling our lives with things that are not of God or from God. I am guilty of trying to fill the empty places of my heart with things of this world, and I became captive. Thank God, he showed me (and continues to show me) the way out! If you let Him, he will break the chains and set you free. Just don't run back and shackle yourself again and be defined by your captivity.

And greater still, take time to give God the glory for releasing you into a life that can be great. As Paul and I read through Exodus recently, I just sat there and couldn't believe how much complaining these people were doing after Moses, through God's might, had been able to free the slaves from the hands of the Egyptians. Then it hit me, another epiphany, "Wow, this is me everyday"…I may not be complaining that I was better off in "Egypt", but I'm complaining about someone's driving, a meal I got a restaurant, that the grocery didn't have my favorite yogurt or a plethora of other things we could grouch about. How about we try to look at what God has done for us. Remember the dark places we have seen and hope we never see again, because of our deliverance. I can't promise I won't complain, ever again, but I can tell you, I hope to realize when I about to do it and in the scheme of life, is yogurt really that big of a deal?

I know for me, I could let the slavery of all my past mistakes, worries; afflictions hinder me from God's great plan for my life. I think this is why writing and laughing has become so important to me, it brings me closer to God. We could let that pain; heartache and worry bog us down allowing it to make us, and everyone around us miserable. Why should we let "who we were" win out when we have the ultimate intercessor? I am thankful, as the verse says that I can let my mouth be filled with laughter and my tongue "sing" songs of joy. I do this as the Lord continues to do great things for me (and my precious family)! I just want others to laugh with us, or even at us. As long as you are laughing with a joyful heart, God is the giver of the gift and benefactor of this laughter.

God said, "Jaime, that's not your gift"

I don't remember dreams of being an author, or of publishing a book. I remember thoughts of being an actress or a singer! Though others may not have been sold on my potential, I wasn't going to let anyone rain on my parade. I did have one staunch supporter in my Mammaw Evelyn. She let me sit at her kitchen table and compose songs about Jesus and sing them too her. There were some real doozies. After she passed away, we went through her items and bless her heart we found many little pieces of paper with my lyrics on them.

In some ways, I fault her for not telling me how awful I really was, but that was what her son, my Dad was famous for, bursting my lyrical bubble. Plus that woman loved her grandchildren so much, she wasn't going to break my little heart over a song…especially not a song about Jesus! In spite of my lack of talent, in my own mind, I was the next "big thing"…I was an "American Idol" long before we had even heard of the show. Problem was (and still is!), I can't carry a tune in an empty bucket…not that that deterred me from singing my heart out.

For the last, I don't know; say 20+ years I have been involved in music at church and when I was in school. Not because I was particularly talented but because that's what I wanted my gift to be. Recently, I heard loud and clear, about my will when it came to singing, and his will for me. God said, "Jaime, that's not your gift". Now, he didn't tell me to quit singing altogether, because I can sing his praise in tune, out of tune, or with no tune at all. He encouraged me to quiet my spirit and listen to Him as I searched for my gift. I think everyone wants to know what we are good at and how to feel useful.

I'm surprised I didn't realize the lack of singing ability in the 6th grade. That was my first solo and singing debut in front of an audience of more than three or four people (some of which left the room before the music even started). It was my grade school's tribute to President's Day. I had the solo in a lovely song entitled "Cherry Tree Chop". I remember seeing my music teacher just below the stage. I came up on cue to the microphone. I was dressed to look like an older woman…with a shawl and white powder in my hair to simulate I was George Washington's mother, or someone older dame from that era. Anyway, I step up in the spotlight. I can feel, as soon as I open my mouth, no words will come out. I am stuck. That was a first! This was it, my big chance and I was blowing it. I look down to see my music teacher nervously yet enthusiastically trying to direct me and feed me the words to the song. It's useless I have already folded under the pressure. However I think I may recover the last few words of my solo, but the damage had been done. As if that wasn't sad enough…I am now in my 30's and I know all the words…"Little George went out into the yard one day, to see what, he could see. He was bored and didn't know what to play until he found an axe and a cherry tree". Isn't that ironic? The words I couldn't even remember as a youth can roll right off my 30-something tongue and have no value whatsoever. Well I guess it does have value in that I can pass along the little nugget of knowledge I deemed from "Cherry Tree Chop". Go me!

Humor has been a defense of mine since my youth. I never remember feeling particularly attractive as a young girl. Not that I was going to let being plain Jane deter my journey on the road to success, because I of course, was destined for stardom, right? Even with all this RAW and untapped talent I possessed, I still only saw the "ugly duckling" in the mirror. Now, I am not referencing that I am a swan at this point in my life in any way shape, or form. I do, however appreciate the woman God has allowed me to become. To this day, I battle self-image vs. God's image of me. In having said that, about being the not-so-pretty one, I was a bit overweight in high school. I often made jokes about my size to help me cope. Like when people asked me what I wanted to do after high school, I sometimes joked, "Perhaps I will be a comedian, if my modeling career falls through". I wasn't so tall and a bit on the portly side, Wilhelmina and the Ford Modeling agencies were not on my radar, if you get what I'm saying! I felt like, and some days still feel like when standing in front of a mirror, that I was in a funhouse with total distortion staring back at me. God did have other plans for me, and modeling wasn't one of them. I was dismayed and elated all at once.

Aside from not being a beauty queen, I also was very average in the grades department. Neither my brother, nor I were overly ambitious when it came to academics. I excelled in language arts, though this work may not reflect that. But, when it came to mathematics, I all but had a mental block. I remember wanting to walk into every math class, I have ever had and just raise the white flag of surrender. You won, math, it's over; I cannot beat this x over y, minus the square root of z. There were just some things, this old brain of mine could not process, and I was resolved to that. I wasn't necessarily proud of my mediocrity, but I knew it could be worse. Apparently, this was a family trait; Matt seemed to suffer the same affliction, as did Dad. I used to joke, "I'm fine with being average, Matt set the standard so low, and I had to do little to surpass it. Thank you Matt!" That sounds mean, doesn't it? That wasn't my intent; I think it's just harder for some folks to learn than it is others. I didn't need a nudge to succeed; I needed an all out push. It was that way, not just through high school, but on into college too!

Matt also knows that he has strengths that I do not... literally "strength" was one of his strengths. My only defense as a little girl, against Matt, when in battle, was my fingernails. Isn't that sad? I used them as a weapon, I had too. Though I don't make it a habit to quote Darwin, it was survival of the fittest. I suppose if you were an onlooker to our shenanigans, our fights might have resembled something seen on Animal Planet. We genuinely disliked each other, again I think it was because I stole his thunder back in the day, but he might remember events differently, he always does.

What I am about to you tell you will probably sound pretty strange, but up to this point, every thing I have said has probably already been pretty strange, why not add another iron to the fire? I remind you that my brother and I share a birthday. Though I may not have been Matt's favorite childhood present, he wasn't mine either. I could not be a twin, or a multiple. Sharing a womb would be bad enough, you know, not getting your "own space" in there? Well when it came to Matt and I we also had to share birthday cakes and parties, like twins, except we have the three year age difference. This never made me happy. I always thought YOU should feel special on your birthday. I think I always secretly resented my parents for having the same birthday, like they planned it that way for us. They are good, but they aren't that good. One year it was the "Pac-Man" cake. I think Mom made them; there were two cakes that year, one for each of us. I was excited at this because I loved Pac-Man and we would have a cake for our very own. Then it happened. She brings the cakes out…who gets to be the hero Pac-Man? Matt, of course, and what do I get, the evil villain, Ghost. I was not a happy camper. However, Matt having a pink ghost just didn't seem right either, you know? But I didn't care. This was all before I knew Jesus of course.

Matt isn't a big cake fan now. Or so he says…I think it's because I am, he just says the opposite to ruffle my feathers. But it's all in good fun. Nowadays Mom has gotten smart and she let's one of us pick the birthday dinner and the other the dessert selection. Just to spite Matt a time or two I have pondered getting a cake, but now that I know Jesus, that's mean. However prior to this new system Mom has put in place she did buy this one cake that just didn't seem right from the time she took it out of the box. It had cowboy hats on it, lassos and a plastic cake topper that said, "Country Music Fan". Now, up to this point our Mother had known each of us for at least 20 years. This cake seemed more for a rodeo fan than for Matt and I. We joked, "So was that last cake at the bakery". Mom sheepishly looked at us and said, "In the hustle and bustle of getting the food together for dinner, I forgot to order the cake".

Matt and I laughed it off. It was funny. We both do like country music; however the theme didn't really fit us. The story didn't end there. It looked a little more strange because there also flowers dispersed throughout the cake and in a small corner, barely legible read and in tiny cursive read, "Happy Birthday Matt and Jaime". So it seemed like someone got really happy decorating this thing. It was like sensory overload on the eyes, not a square inch to spare on that cake. Mom lifts the cake topper off to cut the cake and low and behold there was MORE writing under the topper, it read, "Happy Birthday Deloris". My Dad sat there, with a straight face and said, "Looks like someone forgot to pick up Deloris' cake". Laughter erupted. To this day, that was the ugliest cake I have ever seen, but still one of my favorites.

Though Matt and I did fight a lot, now our relationship is very good. He is honestly one of my best friends and biggest fans. A couple of years ago he was injured in a terrible accident and I thought we had "lost" him forever. Not to death, but to the condition to which he was plagued. It seemed as bad as death to me. It took his sight, his speech and his quality of life. I remember calling his cell phone just to hear the message on it. He had lost most of his ability to speak and the message was recorded long before his injury. Listening to the message gave me hope. Thankfully, the Lord delivered Matt from his illness, though some after effects do remain. I know many people left him at the cross during his struggle with this illness. You know, as terrible as this situation was for Matt, his wife, children and my parents, some good has come from it. Matt is so loved, by all of us. Including his sister who clawed her way through their childhood! I love you Matt!

When I was almost seventeen, our family received a great blessing (many more would follow), by way of Matt. It was the birth of my nephew Sean, Matt's firstborn child. It was a wonderful gift and great distraction all at once. Focusing on this awesome child helped me focus less on me. I suppose it was even cooler because Sean wasn't my child/ responsibility, my memories of him are…well nothing short of spectacular. He was like the little brother I never had, but always wanted. I enjoyed babysitting him. Teaching him things and learning things from him too. He was such a funny kid. Now he's taller than me, and a teenager.

When he would stay the night at my parent's house, and I still lived, there I recall him saying, "Jaime, I wanna go fweep (sleep)." I would say, "Sean, it's 'I want to go to sleep'". So he would try again, "I wanna go s-fweep". I would again correct him, "Try this, 'I want to go to s-l-eep'". He would try it again, "I wanna go s-wa-fleep". Just when it seemed like a lost cause, those big blue eyes of his looked right up at me and said, "Jaime, I wanna go to bed". He was smart even at that age. When at first you don't succeed, just pick an easier word to say.

It was fun to take Sean anywhere. At least it was for me. He was cute, and you could never tell what was going to come out of his mouth. I remember one Christmas, he couldn't have been much more than three, and Mom and I took him to a Christmas Cantata in another town. This program was spectacular. The choir formed a "living Christmas tree", there were live animals and the set looked like Bethlehem. It was a joy to just sit and take it all in.

As the play began, Sean didn't want to sit next to my Mom or me. We were with a group from our home church. Sean decided to sit in between another mother and daughter. I was to his left, and Mom was to his right. At the beginning of the performance, he was already a little restless so my Mom, being a nurse, reached into her purse pulled and out a pen light to pacify him. We were sitting relatively close to the choir members, second row of the congregation, with an empty front row. After a few minutes of the singing, I begin to notice that some of the choir members looked a little distracted, as if something from the audience was taking their focus away from their "Hallelujahs". I look over and see that my cute little nephew is using the pen light to blind

35

the carolers in the Living Christmas Tree. I whisper, pretty loudly, down to Mom, who is about three people down from me and say, "Get that pen light away from him". Mom, in her Memaw wisdom says, "Sean, you give Memaw that pen light and I will get you a prize" Sean sits indignantly in silence, grasping the pen light for dear life, all the while forcefully shaking his head "NO". This wasn't going to be easy, I could tell. So, Mom goes back to it saying, "Sean honey, please give Memaw that pen light and I will get you a prize". Again, he brings it to his chest and shakes his head, "NO". I'm thinking, she may need to call in for back up on this one, I'm about to die laughing over the situation, so I am of NO help to her. Finally she is about to lose it and says, "Sean you give me that pen or no prize". He then very calmly says, "You give me that prize, and I will give you this pen light". Our entire pew almost missed Jesus' birth because of the laughter that erupted from the wise words of my nephew. Memaw did get the pen light back, and Sean did get a prize but the best part of all was witnessing the life of our Savior that night.

Life is Funny!

I was blessed in that my best friend, Meredith was on this journey of higher education with me. We spent many-a-day trying to figure out who we were and what our futures where to hold. We put so many miles on her little Ford Tempo and later Toyota Tercel. I wasn't much of driver... remember I had a "Shovette" and though Meredith didn't mind to ride in it she always shuttled us about town. We make jokes now about how much she drove. I probably could buy her gas for a couple of years and still not repay all the petro she expended during our trips about town. She and I were inseparable, you didn't see one without the other. I think we even began to look alike we spent so much time together.

We actually were roommates for a couple of years. Let me rephrase that, we signed a lease for a couple of years and were formal roommates. Meredith actually had an apartment at 18 and I bunked there many a night and she, like the sweetheart she is, footed the bill. Bless her heart; she probably thought my name was "Moocher" and not Jaime. Rightfully so! Anyway, as roommates one of my favorite things to do was to make up a catchy answering machine jingle. I must tell you, my personal favorite was when I came up with idea to sing our message to the tune of The Dukes of Hazard. This was absolutely a favorite show of me and Matt as kids. It went a little something like this:

"We're just two good ole' girls, never sittin' at home. Beats all you ever saw, we're never home when you call. Leave your message at the tone…YEE-HAW".

Oh how I miss the days of answering machine jingles! Now all I have is a "formal" voicemail message! You might be thinking, right about now…Lisa WAS RIGHT…this girl is certifiably country!

During college, I also really "met" my husband, Paul. You be saying, "really met?", but I did know a him a little bit before we began dating. We grew up in neighboring towns and went to the same middle and high school. Even stranger than all of that would be that, we actually went to the same babysitter as toddlers. Isn't that crazy? Who would think you would marry someone that you went to the same sitter with? I tell you, when we told Ms. Betty, our sitter, she thought it was great. The older I get, the more I appreciate the irony in our relationship. I could write a whole book on that but I am sure the best chapters are yet to come in our life. I remember his mother Marsha and his sister Shannon saying something that I don't think I have appreciated like I should, until lately…and that was that Paul and I "compliment" each other. He's much more introverted than I am, and he gives me a balance that I couldn't achieve on my own. I finally get what Marsha and Shannon were saying, and I value it! As I learn to love like Jesus more and more, I love him more and more!

I would be remiss not to mention some of my favorite laughs Paul and I shared early on in our life together. The day he met my parents is one of my most humbling experiences and one I will never forget. We took a walk around my neighborhood. For some reason he used the word lackadaisical in a sentence. I remember somewhat gaffing at his use of the word. I arrogantly said, "That's not a word", apparently, I thought I was a walking dictionary. He said, "Yes it is", and then calmly gave me the definition. At which point, I puffed out my chest and said, "When we get back to my house let's just ask my Dad". This is because I come from a lineage of walking dictionaries. Paul very calmly said, "That's fine". I couldn't walk fast enough, almost at a sprint, to get back to my house and prove this guy wrong. I bust through the door and almost race to my Dad. I ask him loudly and proudly, "Is lackadaisical a word". I bet you know how this is going to go right? Much to my dismay, my Dad says, "Yes, Jaime, of course it's a word", he then proceeds to tell me the definition, and almost verbatim of what Paul says, "lazy, without effort". NO!!!!!!!!! Thank goodness, Paul didn't go running for the hills after that.

Pretty soon, I got a laugh of my own at Paul's house. It was my first time to meet his family. We arrived to their home before their church had dismissed. Paul was acting as a great host. He asked me if I would like something to drink. I really only drank water at that time, but asked anyway, "What have you got to drink". He then goes down a laundry list of beverages. He pulls a 2-liter out of the refrigerator. I can tell its grape. He then holds it up and says; "This is Lo…lo…" it appeared that he was trying to sound out the name of this cola. Finally, he gets it out and says, "Lo-tasa Cola". I start laughing and say, "Paul, I think that says Lotsa cola". He laughs too and within minutes, the family arrives. I'm intimidated immediately by his Dad, but immediately bonded with my mother-in-law. She and I are laughing and carrying on and I feel it was a good time to share the Lotsa cola story. So I begin telling it, and then I get to the part where he's is sounding it out and says, "Lo-tasa". His

Dad very seriously looks at me and says, "Well Ms. Smarty-pants, what is then?" A hush falls over the kitchen and then, mother-in-law to the rescue, "It's Lotsa, Lotsa Cola, silly". I am almost too afraid to laugh at this point until he begins laughing and says, "Oh, I guess it is". Like father, like son!

When you are dating newly someone, it's nerve-racking celebrating that first birthday together. He doesn't know what to get you, you don't know what to get him, you are still trying to learn each other's likes and dislikes. The first birthday I celebrated while dating Paul was the "Country Music Fan" year…I turned 20. I don't remember what gift he got me. However, there was something very special he did that birthday. I have never forgotten it.

Because Matt and I always had to share birthdays, something that always got to me was that when we had a shared cake (which was about 75% of the time) the greeting on it read, "Happy Birthday Matt and Jaime". Apparently I was greedy…I either wanted my own cake, or my name to come first. In hindsight…and maturity…it only seems natural that Matt's name would come first because he is the oldest. In my "all about me" phase (which lasted far longer than it should have), I wanted a cake with just MY name on it, and had never gotten one, until my 20th birthday. Paul and his family surprised me with my own birthday cake. I remember crying because it felt like they had bought me a new car. That was so special to me. That was the best cake I ever ate. If you are a twin, multiple or you share your birthday with a family member I sure hope the appreciation I had over this cake makes sense to you. If not, for a few years I would like for you to share your cake with someone and put your name last on it. Oh never mind, now that I am grown, it seems so menial to even care.

Matt, I have no problem getting you a cake with your name on it…but since you don't eat cake, I will pick the flavor of my choosing. Kidding! There really is a point to be taken from the cake story. When something is important to someone we love, it doesn't take much to listen to their concerns and give them a "piece" of happiness. I don't do that enough. Just as I have challenged you with that, I now challenge myself.

In my four years, I changed my major once. Unfortunately they didn't have a degree in "Motivational Speaking" so because of this I was undeclared until I was a junior. Initially, though undeclared, I thought maybe I wanted to be on TV. I have no idea why, to be honest. Because of being an insecure and self-conscious person, the thought of being so vulnerable in front of people, more specifically on camera, was pretty stupid. I felt like people would judge me. My teeth, were they straight enough? My eyes, where they too squinty, they sometimes goes away when I smile. What about the weight? They say the camera adds five to ten pounds, that's just what I needed. What was I thinking anyway? I suppose because I thought that's what I wanted to do (until push came to shove) I had to try my hand at it. I quickly learned, through that experience that I really enjoyed radio. You have to focus on the voice and not the face. However, I had classes where I had to be on camera, no choice; it was part of the grade. I remember looking back on the tapes and cringing watching myself. I am from Kentucky so hiding the accent is hard, but that annoyed me too. The way I looked, the way I sounded…everything about it. I remember one "broadcast" in particular; I sounded like a wind-up toy robot. I was very stiff in speaking with somewhat of a "take me to your leader" tone. I ran through the material relatively quickly, barely breathing and then coming to an "out of breath" stop. It wasn't pretty.

After that fiasco, I knew broadcasting wasn't the field for me, however I could speak to a stranger…I could speak in front of people (pretty well)…and I loved interpersonal communication. I stayed in the communications field with an emphasis in public speaking. Am I good at public speaking? Really depends on the day. At best, I guess I am hit and miss because sometimes I hit the mark on what message I am trying to convey and other times I miss and end up shaking my head as I leave the venue (Venue? Like I am playing some big gigs here! I may be at a Senior Center talking about colorectal cancer.). I haven't gotten it perfected, that's for sure, but perhaps that's what makes me real, it will never be perfect. I've learned that is okay, God just wants me to give my best, whether I am speaking to a group or someone one on one. It's not my gift, it's His, given to me to use for His glory and honor.

Well, unfortunately I often interject myself when using my gift of gab. Because of this, my body reacts in a certain way, often. I like to call it "splotchy neck". My neck becomes beet red and I get red splotches (marks that resemble hives… it's really a lovely feature). Pretty much any and every emotion evokes it. My favorite thing is when people point it out. I have been asked, "Are you allergic to something?", "Are you okay?", and "Why is your neck red?" I often try to play it off all cool, but in actuality, talking about it sometimes makes it worse. I sort of feel like the Wizard of Oz, "Please ignore the large red splotches on the neck". What I would like to tell them is, these splotches are like a bug, I feel it crawling up my neck. I had a nice array of turtlenecks at one time. Those worked really well. Or sometimes, I tell them they may need to have their eyes examined because they are seeing red splotches that aren't really there; it's like an optical illusion. Most people don't buy it!

With prayer and resolve, I have just had to come to terms with it. What's cool is to meet another person who gets it too. I have actually made several friends with the affliction. It's nice because we are "sisters" in the "splotch". Shout out to Heather and Jennifer, I love you girls! We understand each other's plight as we each try so very hard, not to be a redneck. Hey ladies, if this is you, and you get red neck too, you can join our club. It's free, but no turtlenecks allowed. We must embrace our splotchiness! Or better yet, if this is you and you have discovered a remedy, share the wealth. I'm pretty sure God has given me the remedy… prayer and release of worry…I just keep trying "my" way and the splotch lives on!

Now you know more than you could ever want to know about me. How about a little more? I'm weird, right? I look like a leopard when I get nervous, only difference is my spots are red and not black. I am a wannabe comedian, with a little material to work from, I've driven some real humdinger cars, what else could there be? Oh, there's more!

The Worry Gene

Believe it or not, someone did actually put me on TV, cable access to be exact. I am honored to be able to co-host a local TV show on the community cable system. Prior to actually being hired for the job, I was interviewed for show. The interview was about our son, whom you will have the privilege to read about in the pages to come. I was a nervous wreck the day of the interview due to previous experiences with cameras. It was anybody's guess how it was going to turn out. In the weeks to follow, the program aired. Paul and I sat down to watch it, with our then, 4-year-old daughter, Brynna. Paul said to Brynna, "Look Brynn, who is that on TV". She pointed at the TV, specifically at me on the screen and said, "A Dork!". I hope that helps you get a clear perspective on why TV is a little difficult for me. My own child thinks I look like a dork.

In my full-time career, I work as a cancer educator. I am required to speak to small and large groups on a regular basis. It is very rewarding, and I say that with much emphasis on very. The men and women I have the pleasure to meet are amazing and inspiring. I think I chose to go into the field of public health hoping that God would use me to bless others for His benefit. However, he never ceases to amaze me by using others to constantly bless me, be it at work or just in my community. I often say, it's not fair to get paid for doing something you love, however don't mistake that as me saying I would work for free. I like getting paid too! But what a blessing when you can go to work everyday at a job you love and reap a paycheck from it. God works through my job, to reach me and make me a better woman.

One woman in particular I've met through my career has given me an entirely new appreciation for life and its circumstances. I will call this gal Judy for the sake of anonymity. What I appreciate most about her is that she has laughed at her life with a big old belly laugh. You know the kind? It's a laugh that starts at the very tip of your toes and begins to well up through the rest of your extremities and before you know it, it has reached your eyes and your laughter is now turning to tears because it's such a cleansing and joyous process. That is how I feel when I'm with Judy. You listen to her and before you know it, she invites you into her funny life and you are seeing things through her eyes. She always starts out a story with, "Life is funny". The longer I have known her it seems the crazier and funnier things are in my in my own life. Or maybe that's not it at all. Perhaps I now I appreciate how she has shared her life and that she can see humor and the hand of God in the most mundane situations. With my own aging here, I am inclined to agree with Judy, "Life is funny".

Judy is a white-haired beauty that seems so unassuming. What I love is that people wouldn't expect more than a sweet grandmother from her and yet she's the one zinging everyone! So before you judge a book by its cover, get their back-story because it could bless your life more than you would ever imagine. I remember the first time I met her I couldn't get enough of her zest for life. I wanted what she had! I wanted to make people laugh, like she does. I think the most beautiful thing with her is she isn't laughing at the expense of others, it her own follies that keep everyone in stitches.

Judy has taught me a lot of things. The most of which is the God gives us life to enjoy it. She is a multi-cancer survivor, and yet, she has praised him in the storm. She continues to praise him. Her praise often comes through laughter at life. Judy inspires me because she has faced MANY trials in her years and yet she perseveres. I am sure she has been down and out, and felt down and out, but from what I have seen, she dusts herself off and gets back up and keeps scooting (in her words) for His glory.

He's Still Working on Me

You know I reflected on not feeling particularly beautiful as a young lady, into my college years and even as a grown woman I often struggle. I felt for some reason like my looks played a part as I searched to find what I was "meant" to do in life. I remember just wanting to "motivate" people. However I was hung up on people not listening to me because I wasn't one of the "pretty people". I still had the desire in my heart though to inspire. So, in response to, "What do you want to be when you grow up" I would with all seriousness say, "I want to be a motivational speaker". Only for NO ONE to take me seriously and quote the famous words from Saturday Night Live skit with Chris Farley where he was mocking motivational speakers and say, "I live in a van down by the river". AAAAHHHH! I love being funny but I did want someone to take me seriously.

Women are mean! Have you ever noticed that? I mean we love to build someone up, just to tear them down. When I was a teenager I was ridiculed one time by a group of girls for my eye makeup. I am sure I was ridiculed for much more than that during my teen years; however this is something that has stayed with me. Almost every day, as I apply my make-up I think about what those girls said. That was almost twenty years ago. In the same token I think about things I might have said to others to hurt them. I don't like being talked about or judged, so why I have subjected other "innocent" people to the same fate? Cause I am a sinner!!!

What does the bible say? Those who guard their tongues keep themselves from calamity (Proverbs 21:23) Okay, I think I can do that, and make a conscious effort to guard my tongue and refrain from negative talk. It's really all about surrender, die to self. Speaking your mind isn't all it's cracked up to be really. Especially if the end goal is to hurt someone and remember this happens unintentionally too. I have done it more times that I can count, however if I guard my tongue then I much less likely to let everything that comes to my mind hit the air.

I was driving to work one morning and I heard a piece of wisdom I wished I would have heard in my youth. Listening to a syndicated Christian radio station a lady spoke about our insecurities as people, but especially as women. I know for me, this talking too much, in the past, has come from me not liking who I am, and has very little do with anyone else but me. She basically said that not knowing exactly who we are and being insecure can help us love other women (people) more easily. We can have empathy for them in their time of need. I felt like someone had hit me upside the head with a frying pan. That was some good stuff! We could look at our insecurities as a blessing from our Creator. Then maybe, just maybe with that realization it's because of those insecurities, we are more able to love unconditionally. Now that was beautiful too me.

I think about "our daughters". My poor girl doesn't have a prayer having me as her mother. My Mom wasn't overly concerned with fashion and hair, so I have no idea where my ideologies and insecurities came from. I do remember her saying things about her figure that bothered me. She and I have had conversations about this as I have gotten older. I remember growing up, being shaped just like her, so I would reflect her negative views of herself onto me because I looked like her. She had NO intent for that to be directed towards me. However in my human mind I took it personally.

I hope my daughter knows I think she is a precious and beautiful gift from God, not just because I tell her so, but because the word of God says. There is a scripture that I am growing to appreciate a little more every day.

1 Peter 3:3-4 (New International Version)

³Your beauty should not come from outward adornment, such as braided hair and the wearing of gold jewelry and fine clothes. ⁴Instead, it should be that of your inner self, the unfading beauty of a gentle and quiet spirit, which is of great worth in God's sight.

As my insecurities have often focused around my personal appearance scripture plainly tells me I should be much more concerned with my "inner self". Imagine if we took this scripture more literally and turned ourselves inside out. There are many times the thought of that is much more frightening that what I have looked like on the outside. WHOA! I have been very ugly in my heart. God sees that and knows my heart; I should be much more concerned with that. I'm reminded as I read it to foster that "quiet" time with God and let him guide my priorities. This makes me much more aware about will or will not leave my mouth from now on. As you can see I am not so good at being quiet! In fact, I talk for a living, for hobby, for sport, for communication, in all things! Jesus take the wheel! Just like the old children's song reminds me, "He's still working on me, to make me what I oughtta be...how LOVING and PATIENT He must be, He's still working on me". AMEN!

Do You See What I See?

A story that I never get tired of telling, or should I say re-telling because Paul thought it was funny long before I did, was of my laser eye surgery. Several months after our first child was born, I just had this "need" to check into laser eye surgery. I had been legally blind since my tweens, so I longed to just wake up in the morning and be able to view the numbers on my alarm clock. Seems like a simple enough request, but for those of you who can't see, like me…you completely understand this longing. I had corrective eyewear since the third grade. Luckily, there was an ophthalmologist who was now performing these procedures in town. So, like any other legally blind vain woman (we have already established that I fight vanity), I got an appointment with the doctor as soon as they could fit me in.

The appointment was rather uneventful. They examined my eyes, made me watch a video, told me I was a candidate and we then scheduled a date for the surgery. Simple enough! This was going to be great!

The day of the surgery, you had to have a designated driver because you were required to rest your eyes for an extended period of time. That was no problem, and Paul was able to oblige. Dad also had the procedure done that day. Mom called me to let me know how he fared but also to share a little insight with me. I welcomed it, because I was scared. I was already legally blind as it was the thought of it not working or having permanent eye damage did cross my mind. I'm so optimistic aren't I? Mom told me that it might be wise to take a Valium, it is offered at the physician's office. This will obviously help to calm those nerves that accompany any surgery.

When I arrived, the Valium was offered. I can't recall if Mom directed me to take a whole or a half of the pill. However, I felt REALLY nervous so I thought a whole one would do the trick. Oh, it did a trick, alright. I don't think I had ever taken a Valium up to that point in my life. I had quite the reaction to it. I cried like a baby. Now, I am not talking about upset crying, with an emotion attached too it. I just began crying, like someone turned on the waterworks and couldn't shut them off. The staff asked me if I was okay, and I kept insisting, "I am not upset", all the while I look like a comic strip with water shooting out of both eyes like a sprinkler system. My words and actions did not match up.

Because of this slight problem, they were unable to operate with my tear ducts working overtime. So they took a couple of patients before me. This allowed me to "calm" down and give the old eyes a needed rest. Finally, the tears stopped and I was smiling, I mean really smiling because it was my turn to get these eyes fixed, once and for all!

The surgery goes off without a hitch. After it was complete, they bandage the eyes. Because I couldn't see what I looked like, I am only imagining here, but I would say I probably looked like an insect. Not a bad look for me, I'm sure, but also not a preferred look. With the bandages in place, they also added a pair of large sunglasses to shield my eyes further from the elements. The staff then gives Paul specific instructions on how to care for my eyes that evening. At that, we are ready to exit the building.

I am feeling good, though I can't see due to the bandaging, I feel good about what had just happened. Paul takes me by the arm and away we go. I guess I should say, away he goes! In order to exit the building you must go back through the waiting room. My eyes are bandaged and I cannot see a thing. It was like walking around with your eyes closed and your hand then covering them. He begin to pick up his pace and is walking like a mall walker, you know the kind, they go to your local mall and make like 15 laps at an unbelievable rate of speed as your dodge them just to get your next shopping destination? Yeah, he was walking at a crazy fast pace. I then begin to plead with him, "Slow down, slow down, I can't see, I can't see". He begins "shushing" me with urgency. I feel like I am going to fall and he seems to be going even faster, to which I say again, "Slow down, slow down, I can't see!" He shushes even louder. At this point, I can feel we have reached the door and he opens it for me. We are in the parking lot and Paul just busts out in laughter. I, feeling a bit sorry for myself at this point say to him, "Why wouldn't you slow down, you know I can't see right now! That really scared me. It's not funny, why are you laughing??" Through his unstoppable laughter he says, "Jaime, you just walked through a whole waiting room full of people waiting to have the very same procedure done, and you are ranting like a crazy person, 'I can't see, I can't see'. You sure are great advertising for them. You should have seen the looks on those people's faces. It was priceless". I was so embarrassed, but for the first time I think I had truly experienced, "out of sight, out of mind". I just wanted to get home! However, I really would have liked to have "seen" the looks on their faces. Lucky, Paul!

Parenting: A Puzzling Experience

I love good humor; I think its medicine for the soul. A gift God gives to show his people his goodness through the slightest things in life. This humor has helped so much in our lives as parents. I'll tell you why I, and my husband, specifically need and appreciate the laughter in our lives. When our oldest child, Beau, was born in 2001, it was one of the HAPPIEST times for Paul and me. The pregnancy and delivery were almost effortless (Mom, if you are reading this please do not recant some of the delivery room antics I was told I spewed under the spell of a painkiller that will remain nameless). It was good to be me. While pregnant, I can truly say, I felt like the MOST BEAUTIFUL woman in the world. If I wasn't, I didn't want to hear about it, as you can see; humility is not my strong suit. Again, I will remind you this is my version of events. The day he was born, Paul and I went for what would end up being our final visit before Beau was delivered. My doctor asked if I would like to come back to the hospital in a couple of hours and have the baby, he felt Beau was ready to make his grand appearance. We left the office just overjoyed and a bit scared. We get into the elevator to ride down to the lobby and this "happy" woman gets on the elevator. She was smiling as much as we were, I think! She looks at me and says, "Oh look at you, did you just find out you were having a baby". I probably had a dumbfounded look on my face…people I was nine months pregnant! I said, "Sort of, we are going to the hospital in a couple of hours to deliver our baby". I then "proudly" turned sideways and showed off my baby hump… it had passed bump about three months prior. Up to that point, I can't recall ever being happier as I was on that day, the day of his birth.

Beau physically had all the right parts in all the right places. As his young life progressed, issues emerged…almost immediately. I remember thinking, "my pregnancy was ideal, why isn't this baby?" I suppose it's because we live in a faulty and imperfect world, full of imperfections. You know the world where people have problems and some babies have health concerns, and our son did. Though I will say he looked perfect too me and to Paul. However, I will always be biased that my babies were the prettiest babies ever born. Just like yours!

First, though later it wouldn't prove to be such a big deal, it was huge to a first time mother and father. Beau was diagnosed with the birth defect pyloric stenosis at 3 weeks old. With the diagnosis came a surgery on the very same day to repair the defect. I won't bore you with details of that…search it and I am sure you can find more than you would like to know about it. Praise God it was a repairable ailment.

After his surgery, it was repeated trips to the hospital for the next few months. It really seemed like if you even so much as sneezed around this kid, he would get sick. We joked that Halloween that we would dress him as a patient because he had a lovely selection of hospital gowns from his frequent stays. We also wondered if the pediatric wing of the hospital would have a room named in his honor due to all the money we shelled out that first year of his life. We felt like that was the least the hospital could do. Apparently, they didn't agree, he never got his own room. Bummer! Luckily, he's never made it back there, not since 2001. Praise God!

Oh, did I mention his disposition? WOW, he was really friendly...cried every time his eyes were open. I know individuals who were nicknamed "Smiley" because of their precious disposition as babies; Beau's would have been more like "Sour Puss"...doesn't quite roll off the tongue like "Smiley". He just didn't seem to really bond with anyone, me the most, but didn't even really seem particularly crazy about his own Momma. There were people in our lives that would try to take Beau when he was crying. I guess they felt like they had the "magic touch", or felt bad for him because he seemed so unhappy. I would sit back, hand him off, and just watch as the concerned person tried to pacify my crying baby. To no avail, Mommy or Daddy would always get him back within minutes. We decided early on in Beau's life, not to be offended when someone would offer to take him and try to calm him down. We knew, he would be right back in our arms whaling and fussing again and that was okay. He was safe with me and his Daddy, we didn't care, and we loved that little stinker, crying and all. He was our boy! You could say, Paul and I weren't really "welcomed" into parenthood. I would say it was more like we were catapulted at an alarming rate of speed. We just did what any other unassuming young parent would do. We put our safety belts on and braced for impact.

Looking back, time went by rather quickly, though some days with a fussy and/or sick child feels like an eternity. Some "impacts" were worse than others. Even as fast as time seemed to slip away we noticed Beau wasn't progressing like other babies born around the same time, and he often "slipped away" into his own little world. We were not in the habit of comparing him to other children. These were just noticeable and more obvious differences. We started feeling a tugging in our hearts that something was wrong… developmentally.

So what did we see? Well, with our little man there no words…talk about heart breaking for me. People would often say, "Oh Jaime, he doesn't have to learn to talk, you talk enough for the both of you". OUCH! However, I did think they may be right. He was late walking, made no attempts to walk or crawl until he was about 18 months old. He was happiest in a swing, a baby swing. I bet, to this day, he would still sit in it if we let him. He loved to swing or rock back and forth. He showed no interest in playing with other kids, that was a tough pill to swallow for Momma because she is a social butterfly, Daddy found it strange though too. Beau liked toys, but didn't play appropriately with them. He would line them up, to look at them and just become attached to them in spite of having no imaginary play with them. It was just strange.

After playing several rounds of "what could it be", we finally put a name to this "puzzling" behavior…autism. What am I saying? "We"…like Paul and I could diagnose him, yes, "we" are Dr. and Dr. Rafferty. I don't think the public education system would be okay with that, our elementary diagnosis of Beau. We had, after visiting two psychologists, the diagnosis of ASD (Autism Spectrum Disorder). When I speak about autism in public or to other parents who suspect a child may have autism, I immediately tell people not to search everything out on the internet; this is for a myriad of reasons. The "answers" your search yields could either scare you half to death, or give some people false hope. I'm not suggesting that you necessarily take my approach either. Paul deals with it differently that I do. My best defense is to joke, so I use the analogy if I had a stomachache today and went on the internet with a laundry list of symptoms I could diagnose myself with ulcerative colitis by the time I turn my computer off and simply have a case of gas. Will worrying, with or without an answer add any days to your life? No. I think I lost a few days, probably a few weeks over wondering what was wrong with Beau. Seek spiritual guidance from the Almighty and professional advice from people in the field. Worrying about autism doesn't change Beau's diagnosis. We feel like being proactive and learning him and his needs will help us succeed. Take each thing as it comes. Autism is not the end of the world for my family.

It may be odd to some people, but it just seemed natural to use the same humor to deal with the autism. Like when people who were going to deal with Beau in daycare, church, or an after school program some would say, "Oh, I've never cared for a child with autism". I would laugh and say, "Us either, until Beau came along". I wanted them to feel okay with Beau's autism, because like it or not, we really have had no choice to be okay with it. He's our son and we love him, with or without autism. Plus, it doesn't necessarily define him, though we realize it is a huge part of our lives at times.

I will let you in on Beau's diagnosis. He is considered to have high functioning autism. We do feel very good about that diagnosis. However, with that "high functioning" lingo some people meet and expect more, and some people just don't know what to think. Beau is just Beau and that's what makes him so special. He is able to speak, sometimes more than even, I am prepared for and I love it. I think people are scared, not knowing or understanding autism, whether it's Beau or any other person and I can appreciate that. Paul and I weren't necessarily scared of it, because it was our child that was affected but I would say we were more unprepared that scared. That's where faith comes in, and our faith is that God has a purpose for every single life he created. It's up to us to be available to be vessels or vehicles for him to use. Life is full of twists and turns and to look at Beau, people may not have a clue that he even has autism. We have had our share of stares, uncontrollable meltdowns in grocery stores and fixations on things that result in stimming (hand flapping and/or rocking). If you ever meet me, and I look familiar, it may because one of the "grocery store meltdowns" or perhaps it was a "super center meltdown" and I too was laying of the floor throwing a tantrum because I didn't know what to do to get Beau to stop. I'm laughing as I write this. Beau often uses a phrase he's picked up from one of his favorite shows, it seems pretty fitting as I describe me doing this in the middle of store, "Now that's something you don't see everyday!" Think about it, a grown woman, with nothing developmentally known to be wrong with her thrashing about on the floor. I would like to think if I did this it wouldn't be because I felt helpless but more to take the focus off my baby and just let the people stare at me. I'm a big girl, I can handle it. No wait a minute, I am really not good at all handling it, that's why I would be lying on the flooring throwing my own tantrum. The great thing is the grace of God continues to see us through all the tantrums, our's and Beau's. Woo-hoo!

This autism journey, it's going to be a long one, he is only eight (almost nine), and already it has been one of the biggest learning experiences of our lives. Though I wouldn't have chosen to have a child with autism, God chose Paul and me to parent this child with autism. Ever heard the saying, "God knows what he's doing?" we felt, and many days still feel, that was questionable at best. Surely, God could have chosen two more patient parents than his Dad and me! I am sure glad he didn't though. I think there have been lessons along the way I could have only learned through being Beau's mom. I humbly say, we must completely trust in God's will and plan for Beau. I trust in His plan for both my children.

We did consider that God had challenged us when we found out Beau had autism. It's not like we were elated that our son was "different". Paul and I both faced our own inner battles with the diagnosis, and we still do. We are human and our expectations of each other, though often unrealistic, we have them. We had the expectation that our son would be, by society's standard, "normal". I guess when I think about it now, society is pretty whacked out on many of it's ideologies about people and life, so Beau's normal should be great for us. Looking back what we didn't realize was that autism was ironically a piece of the puzzle for our family and that Beau and Brynna (too) would fit perfectly into our family. The puzzle piece represents the symbol for autism. Man, is that a great "fit", because sometimes just as we think we have the "puzzle" figured out, it's not the right "piece" for Beau.

I love how God uses scripture to speak to us, when we are confused or feel a little lost about circumstances in our life. I try, though I often fail. Paul and I wouldn't be doing Beau any favors if we allow the autism to dictate his success for the future or for our future as a family. That's just saying that God can't do magnificent things. Beau doesn't even know what autism is, hopefully he never knows or understands. If he thinks, he has a disability he may never see his amazing abilities. As the old saying goes, "God doesn't choose the qualified, he qualifies the chosen". AMEN! This was never more clear to me than in reading:

2 Corinthians 12:9-11 (New International Version)

⁹But he said to me, "My grace is sufficient for you, for my power is made perfect in weakness." Therefore, I will boast all the more gladly about my weaknesses, so that Christ's power may rest on me. ¹⁰That is why, for Christ's sake, I delight in weaknesses, in insults, in hardships, in persecutions, in difficulties. For when I am weak, then I am strong.

Sometimes our earthly "fight" with things in life can be so overwhelming. But scripture reminds me I am weak on my own, he's preparing us in his glory through our difficulties. Autism, for our family, can be a witnessing tool for the Lord. Not to mention, we ALL go through tough times. We are not alone in our hardships. All people experience less-than-ideal circumstances, it how we react to them that can set us apart.

I Think This Family Needs a Break

Did I mention (a mere 21 months after Beau was born), we had a daughter…talk about a beauty and talk about a God-thing. This baby girl, Brynna, had a demeanor that was polar opposite of her precious older brother. Everything that Beau wasn't, she was. She slept soundly from the first night she arrived home from the hospital, would let anyone hold her and only cried when she needed to be fed or changed. I think you get the idea. I often wondered if she were an alien, or if God just said, "I think this family needs a break!"

Actually, the decision came about in a couple of ways. First, one of my dearest friends found out she was pregnant with her second child, her son was only 6 months old. I felt like she didn't want to be pregnant alone. I was a good sport and told her maybe I would get pregnant too. I went home, talked to Paul, he didn't mind and wouldn't you know it, I was pregnant by the next month. I don't remember fully consulting with God on this decision as we probably should have however, His hand was in it. The reason we say this is because Paul and I both know we may not have had another child in fear that they too might have the difficulties that Beau had. So not really taking time to go through all the "what ifs" and going out on faith seemed the best choice. Praise God, it did work out for His glory and my sweet friend and I got to blow up like balloons together.

Brynna was a Godsend from the beginning. I love how people have opinions though, it's kind of funny. Paul and I made the decision to try for another baby, yes, it was the same month Beau turned one. But I guess I failed to realize they were going to have a hand in raising Beau and this other baby, at least that's what their "concern" implied. If that was the case, then I sure was glad to have all the help I could get!

The blessed and best thing with Brynna was that we didn't necessarily need the help of people who thought we were crazy having this second baby when we already had a baby. Her pleasant disposition was welcomed by everyone she came into contact with, including her Mommy and Daddy. I referenced what a beautiful baby she was. Oh goodness, physically she was just breathtaking. I'm really not just saying that, I mean it! Gorgeous! I can take NO credit for this. After they were born, I would question whether the two little dolls sent home with us were switched at birth with "my babies". They absolutely looked and still look nothing like their mother. I have joked that I was just the incubator. I can remember the nights before their births, lying in bed just picturing what they would look like. God has a wonderful sense of humor. I'm a brown hair, brown-eyed girl. I always thought my children would get those dominant genes of mine. For some reason I didn't really take Paul's genes into consideration when I was carrying our babies. He has jet-black hair and hazel eyes. I mean, I am their mother; it's only natural that the children I birth will be mini-me's, right? Uh, NO! I couldn't have been more wrong if I tried. Both of my beautiful children don't even look like me, in the slightest, in my opinion. Probably not a bad thing, we've already established a modeling career wasn't even an option at any point in my life. So what do they look like? These kids have hair in the blonde family and blue eyes. I always wanted blue eyes; I'm living vicariously through them now.

I remember as a little girl people saying that I actually did favor my mother. I couldn't fully appreciate it until I got older. Paul and I have looked at pictures of her when she was in her twenties and one might think it was me... though I am no longer in my twenties. I think it really hit me the other night when I was washing my face and brushing my teeth. I had my hair pulled back in a clip. I was rinsing my mouth out, and threw my head backwards and almost screamed. I thought, "Mom when did you get here, you weren't invited". In actuality, I was looking at myself in the mirror. Nice! My mom is a beautiful woman, inside and out, but I didn't expect to morph into her as I aged. I should have paid more attention to her in her 30's and 40's to give me an idea of how this whole aging thing is going to go down for me. I will say she looks great in her 50's, so I'm thinking I'm going to turn out just fine in that area. I don't think this will ever happen to Brynna since we don't even look like we are related on most days. Lucky girl!

Kids Say the Funniest Things

As my kids began to grow up, I began jotting down these little cutesy things they would say to me and too each other. I think the first "story" I kept record of was Brynn and I playing what I called the Animal Game.

One day while laying on the couch my precious little Brynna, age three, is playing the "Animal Game". She names an animal and I must then give the corresponding sound, which that animal makes. This should be easy right? For the average Mom yes, but for me, not as easy. I am one of these people who have a case of self-diagnosed ADHD. My mind is often either three steps ahead, or four steps behind what is going on at the moment. Just like with Brynna's animal game.

Brynn decides to start with a relatively easy one, the chicken. I can do this! So I begin to give my best cluck. To which I receive a rousing, "Yay, Mommy" from my sweet girl. We are then on to other birds. So, my dear Brynna then says, "Do a ducky". I am then quacking with the best of them, and also interject my Donald Duck impression (Dad thanks for honing that gift in me!). Again, I receive a rousing applause for my performance. This is great, I'm thinking!

Things get a wee bit harder. Next, we go into the cat family…tiger, lion, etc. I don't know about you, but I find it hard to differentiate one sound from the next! So for all of them, I keep it safe and just sort of mix a roar and a growl. The growl was also used for the bear. I never claimed to be good at this "Animal Game".

Then it just got weird. She says, "Spider". I'm thinking… okay this is getting a little ridiculous and I'm ready for it to be OVER. I sit there…pondering the noise of a spider. All I can do is lay there, put my fingers in the air, and do what sounds like sort of a hissing sound. It is outright pitiful! Again, she says, "Spider, Mommy". And I again give my little hissing/finger impression. Finally, she SCREAMS points beside my head and says "No Mommy, SPIDER". I look over and right beside my left eye…on the pillow beside my head is what looks like a tarantula… it was a huge spider.

So what's the lesson here? I'm not sure there is one, but when your kid says spider…just to be cautious, look around and know that there is not really a good impression for one like there is for cat or dog and other animals. Better yet just to be on the safe side believe them, they may not be the "little boy who cried wolf". It may be there way of alerting you are about to become acquainted with an arachnid, up close and personal!

Kids are just so literal, and I suppose under certain circumstances, like the Animal Game this is a good thing. I took Beau to K-Mart for some swimming supplies, and he wanted a toy. Beau is definitely a literal child too. Well his behavior reports this week were very good at autism camp and the YMCA, so I decided to oblige. He chose…picture it if you will…a Mr. Potato Head Transformer; yes, it is quite a sight. For those familiar with the Transformers, he is actually Optimus Prime Mr. Potato Head...anyway.

He wanted to take his new toy to his friend Carson's house to show him off. I said, "Buddy, you will lose the pieces". He said, with insistence, "No, I won't,

no, I won't!" I said, "It's new, and I don't want it too be lost". I thought that was that...so then I hear some rustling around of items, and I thought to myself, he has gotten a baggy out of the drawer to put the loose pieces in, how grown up. But, then I feel a tug at my shirt, and he says, "Mom, Mom"..."He's fine". I look and all Mr. Potato Head is wearing is his robot (Transformer) arms, and Optimus Prime "helmet". I said, "What did you do with the rest of him, the other pieces?" Beau says, "He's fine, he's fine". Then smilingly, with the Mr. Potato Head's rear towards me and says, "All his parts are in his butt".

It took me a minute, and then I realized, Mr. Potato Head has a back flap for his parts, and it located on his posterior...but all Brynna could say was, "Oooh Beau, that's gross! We don't put things in our butts." Oh, what fun it is too be raising my two little Raffertys!

Paul and I should have stuck with simple toys for the kids, much longer than we did. It was far easier to get Optimus Primes helmet out of a flap on the back of a Potato Head than some of the things we have had to deal with now. We have found out the hard way that kids and TV's that do more than just have a picture and an off/on button are too much for our children. I suppose it really isn't a good idea to let your kids have electronics at such a young age. This epiphany didn't hit me with mine until they both already had more gadgets than me and my husband. Late one night in the evening air Paul and I hear the screech of our baby girl Brynn crying uncontrollably and a whizzing noise like I have never heard before. We thought it had to be bad because our bedroom is across the house from her room. Paul and I rush to her rescue. I sit down on her bed; she has BIG crocodile tears running down her sweet cheeks. Through the tears, she manages to muster up,

"I put 2 DVD's in my DVD player, I'm really sorry". Paul opens the DVD player to find to DVD's buzzing around, but virtually unharmed. Her dad asks her to select one, she does, and he puts it on for her. He exits the room, she lies down and says...and I quote, "Mommy, tell daddy thank you, I really thought that thing was gonna blow". Apparently, our DVD player was much more resilient than any of us would ever give it credit for. Let's just hope she remembers to remove a DVD before she decides to put a second one it again. Who knows, next time, it really could blow!

Because I Said So!

Like many Americans we have been pulled into the lure that is reality TV. During one of our weekly Dancing with the Stars viewings, Brynna decides to join the living room family festivities. As two of the popular dancers come on the screen she looks at me, while pointing at the screen with one hand, and the other hand perched upon her hip and says, "Mom, her dress is SO TACKY. Do you like it?" I said, "Well there isn't much of it." She says, "I know, it is SO TACKY, she needs more dress." After giggling at her perception of the DWTS fashion, we continue to watch the show. Two more dancers enter the ballroom and she says, "Mom, how about her dress." I said, "It is

really pretty, I like it, do you?" She says... "Yeah it isn't actually (she loves saying actually) TACKY like that other girls dress". Of course, she is laughing all the while because she thinks she is such a big girl...with big words.

Makes me wonder when she's going to realize her Mommy isn't the fashion maven she thinks she is. I'm sure one of these days, much sooner than I'd like, I'm the one that's going to hear, "Mom, YOUR dress is SO TACKY". At which point I may have to evoke parental control and pull out the infamous phrase, that I've always wanted to use, "I brought you into this world, and I can take you out". God be with us!

Beau, has apparently been watching too much TV too because he also likes to be at the height of fashion. One year for Halloween, he wanted to be Optimus Prime from Transformers. Unfortunately, due to popular demand, I absolutely could not find Optimus anywhere in town. Paul and I were ready with a back up plan in place, so his second choice was Superman. I luckily found the Superman costume pretty close to Halloween, and the costume was already 25% off. I bring it home and Beau goes absolutely crazy over it. We take it out of the bag and put it on him. He walks over to the full-length mirror on the bathroom door. As he is admiring himself he says, "I'm not Beau, Beau is gone...I am Superman." Paul isn't home to appreciate or to witness the hysterics of Beau's reaction to his new costume. I asked Beau to come over to me so I can adjust the "belt" on the costume, he looks back at his reflection and says to the mirror, "Don't worry, I'll be back". This time I am over the moon in laughter. About that time Paul gets home and Beau is more than ready to show him just how big his "super muscles are". He parades around the house in a most majestic manner, intermittently stopping by the mirror to catch a glimpse of the "man of steel" and flexing his muscles ever so discreetly. So, if you were looking for Beau and he seemed hard to find that year, he dropped the alter ego after Halloween. If you might have seen him, he probably denied it and told you, he was not Beau; he was none other than SUPERMAN! At least that was word around the house!

Brynna isn't so much the "super hero" kind. She is more of a "realist" at heart. Always asking questions that I either can't answer or my response is uproarious laughter. I was really taken aback by a question she posed one day after we had dropped Beau off at school. Out of the clear blue, with no warning she says, "Can I have a little sister and Beau have a little brother". I just rolled my eyes, but played along. I asked her nonchalantly what would she name this phantom baby, she said, "Sarah Layne". I thought that was so cute wanting to give her that middle name especially since her name is Brynna Layne. After a brief pause I said, "Oh I love that name, Sarah Layne Rafferty". She said, "No Mom, it's Sarah Layne Brown, I didn't say anything about her having MY last name". I mean, what was I thinking; Brown is the only logical choice for a last name of a baby born into our family, right? In the same breath, after naming baby Sarah Brown she utters out of the blue, "I just love McDonald's coffee"...she is just so worldly. Her father and I lavishly shower her with McDonald's coffee and bring children into our home that we let her name. She really is our little princess.

Perhaps Brynna's baby fever came from seeing others family's around us having babies. As we drove up to Beau's grade school, I saw his teacher who was VERY pregnant standing in the student drop off line waiting to assist him in exiting the car. I said aloud, but really just talking to myself, "Ms. Colbert is about ready to pop". Beau said, "Pop?" Forgetting he probably didn't understand what I said I rephrased with a more kid friendly sentence. "Beau, Ms. Colbert is getting ready to have a baby." He said, "Where is it?" I said, "It's in her belly", he said, "What happened, did she eat it?" I am not one to be left speechless, but I will just let that one speak for itself!

After dropping Beau off at the grade school one morning, Brynn and I are driving through what Brynna calls "the woods" around a local country club. We were in route to her day care. This particular morning was not ideal for anything outside, including driving. There was and abundance of rain, lightening and thunder. All of a sudden came a flash of lightening with a crash of thunder and Brynna, out of shock and surprise...very seriously says, "Who took that picture?" in an exasperated and taken aback "What'choo talkin' bout' Willis?" voice.

I begin to try to explain the process of lightening. I pretty quickly got over my own head with a less-than-scientific explanation. I gave up and said, "Honey, God took the picture". Then comes the question about thunder... but that was much easier to explain...God moving furniture. No wonder my parents were exhausted by the time Matt and I reached our teen years! Kids ask way too many questions and I have a whole new appreciation for the phrase, "Because I said so!"

I Love You, Meme!

I'm one of those "weird" people who think of all people, celebrities included, as just people. Now, having said that, if Billy Graham, Beth Moore or Kay Arthur walked into my church on Sunday I would be so humbled and star-struck I would either be rambling or speechless. I'm sure if my family is reading they would say, "Oh she'd be rambling", they are probably right. But to get to the point, I believe the bottom line is that people are people. So with that in mind, in the fall of 2007 I wrote to the Dr. Phil Show with conviction that it would much appreciated if he would do a show on autism. As an autism parent, it is in some strange way, reassuring to know there are other families with the same struggles. My thinking was, Dr. Phil reaches so many homes not affected by autism, I think they need to see what struggles, confusion and blessings (too) that we face that maybe different then having children with normal development. If the numbers are accurate and as many as 1 in 70 boys being diagnosed with autism, then there is a very good possibility in your circle of family, friends and community members that you will have an encounter with a person who has autism sometime in your life.

One weekend, I was working at a breast cancer survivor's retreat when I received and e-mail from the Dr. Phil Show. I almost fell out of my chair in disbelief that someone actually read my message and agreed. Though I calmly acted as if I could just e-mail the show and tell them my views, I think in my heart I never expected a response. Apparently, there were others like Paul and I who wanted to see the same thing, a show about our families and our lives with autism. They asked if I could send photos of our family and if I would be available via telephone to record a brief interview. Without hesitation, I asked Paul, and we agreed to be a part of this show in Beau's honor.

The producer, Ingrid phoned me the following week to record. I was a nervous wreck. I remember sitting in the driveway at my grandparent's home when they phoned. My voice shook as I spoke. I hoped I was capturing the heart of every parent I knew and even those I have yet to meet, or never meet, that had a child or family member affected by autism. But, I knew that was impossible. In addition, I wanted to be sensitive to the needs of other "autism families" too. Just like with every other child, all children with autism are so different, I didn't want my responses to seem one size fits all.

As a couple of weeks passed, I received an e-mail from the show letting us know when it would play. In our area, the show airs at 3pm. Because I work full-time, my program assistant and I went to my grandparent's house to watch it. The show was lovely, just beautiful. My Grandmother, Betty, is probably where I get my chattering from; no, I can almost assuredly say that is where I get my chattering from. She too can talk to a brick wall. Not something either one of us are super proud of, but it is what it is. She is, in fact so chatty, that she talked during our entire segment of the Dr. Phil Show, which was all of about 10 seconds. Yes, I missed the Rafferty family national TV debut. Did I get mad? Nope, I laughed my head off, and imagined myself, at her age, doing the very same thing. Thank goodness, my Grandfather was taping it in the other room. My assistant and I walked calmly to the spare room, without Meme and watched it uninterrupted. I did learn a lesson from this; don't go to her house if you are afraid you have got something really important that you don't want to miss! As I witnessed, there is a good chance you will miss it if she has something on her mind. I love you, Meme!

Santa Shops at Wal-Mart

I love being with both my kids, don't get me wrong, but sometimes it's so nice to be able to dedicate time to just one of the kids. My favorite way to do this is at the grocery store. During a routine Mother/Son trip to Wal-Mart with Beau, we end up in the deli section. I was waiting in line to buy a rotisserie chicken. There was a man in front of

me ordering. Beau was looking at me saying, "I'm talking to you, I'm talking to you". I could hear him jabbering but he wasn't really saying anything, or at least that was the way it appeared to me. I finally realized he had been trying to strike up a conversation with a stranger but was looking at me. Though I wish he wouldn't try to speak to strangers, this was huge for me and really good for Beau because at this time he rarely initiated conversations. However, I wanted to see what my little guy was trying to communicate to this man, when I notice something special for myself about this man and said, "Beau, who does he look like". Beau said very wide-eyed, "Santa Claus"...and he looked JUST LIKE Santa. Let me rephrase that, he didn't have on the red suit and hat, more like flannel and blue jeans, but apart from that, he was a dead ringer for the jolly fellow.

"Santa" just smiled. Beau asked him, "What have you got?" The man politely said, "Chicken". I kid you not, Beau said, "For your wife?" the man then laughed and said, "Mrs. Claus doesn't live with me anymore". He was so funny I couldn't hold back the laughter, though I was very sad to hear he and Mrs. Claus had parted ways. Then Beau says what any normal kid would want to know from the Big Guy, "Are you coming to my house". He said, "If you are good". Beau then throws his sister straight under Santa's sleigh and says, "Brynny is on the naughty list". (She would have smacked him silly if she had heard that. I am assuming Beau said this because Brynna kept asking her Dad and me if she was on the good list. This of course changed daily that year!). The man gathers his chicken from the associate. As he begins to walk away Beau yells, "Don't forget to come to my house".

Everyone standing around the deli had the biggest smiles on their faces...mine included. It was such a great moment for me as his mother. The man was so kind and gentle. I just don't think he realized Beau was talking to him at first but when he did, Beau had his undivided attention. With Beau, his autism seems to most effect him socially, he sometimes not speak directly to you, but I am grateful he does speak...even to Santa. And I can now confirm what people have been contemplating for years, Santa DOES shop at Wal-Mart!

Poor Brynna

It was a Monday night in the middle of winter and Brynna's birthday. The weather in our area was pretty treacherous. Luckily were able to make it to Texas Roadhouse, where she wanted to go for her special dinner. She specifically told us she wanted to go so she could throw peanuts on the floor. Beau's not a peanut eater and we got there he was throwing them on the floor shell and all. I don't think he got it.

For her big elaborate birthday dinner, she orders mashed potatoes and a hotdog. What an appetizing combo, makes you hungry just thinking about it, doesn't it? She tells Paul," I want salt and pepper on my mashy taters". Paul tells her she can pour the pepper because it comes out slower than the salt, which he helps her with. They proceed with the seasoning. About 2 seconds after she pours the pepper on her potatoes she takes the shaker and licks the top of it like a lollipop. In disbelief and disgust I reactively say, "What in the world are you doing?" She smiles and says, "I got a little mashed tater on it and had to get it off". I thought Paul was going to lose it. I'm sure they have sanitized many times since this incident took place. We have been back since the incident in question, and my greatest fear was seeing a "Most Wanted" poster of my daughter upon entering. Thank goodness, she didn't get us kicked out of one of our most favorite eateries.

For the last few years, I have had some minor thyroid issues. I had to have a needle biopsy done at one point on a nodule on my thyroid. Paul went with me as moral support and I needed it. I didn't like it one bit! Because we had taken off half the day for the biopsy something good did come out of it, we were able to pick the kids up earlier than usual. Paul went in the daycare to get Brynna. He told her he had a surprise waiting for

her in the car (ME!). Anyway, she runs out wide-eye and hops in the car. She is smiling a very sweet smile and tells me I am a great surprise. I immediately forgot my thyroid "troubles" after hearing that.

After being so excited to see me, she got very quiet for several blocks. She finally works up the nerve to ask, "Mom, why'd you do it?" I unsuspectingly said, "Do what?" After some serious thinking on her part she says, "Why'd you put 2 pairs of panties on me? Why'd you do it?" I said, "Are you sure?" She tells me yes. Apparently when she went to the bathroom that morning she discovered she was pulling doubles in the panty department. Paul and I were laughing because she was so upset over it but wasn't bothered enough to tell her teachers. I am only assuming that I forgot to take off her bedtime panties. That morning she was so excited about her new Hannah Montana shirt. The only logical explanation is that I just slid the second pair on and didn't notice. To make matters worse I took her and Beau to the gym that night while I took an dance aerobics class. We were getting ready to walk out the door and low and behold, she reminded me she still had on both pair of panties. By that point, I was over the panty debacle, and told, her to suck it up because it was now evening time and she had walked around all day with two pair on, what was another couple hours hurt? My mind goes a million miles an hour, regardless of the time of day so I am not surprised I put two pairs of panties on my girl. In the same token leave it too Brynna to tell me ALL about it! So if your daughter happens to run off and forget her panties, tell them to ask Brynna to help out, because her Mom is a bit of an airhead she might just have a pair to spare.

Where Do They Come Up with this Stuff?

If stories about gas make you uncomfortable, you may want to put this book down now. My children are human and my husband and I are human, so are stories are not scripted and I think that's what makes them so precious too me. I remember one morning Beau was sitting on my lap as I ate my granola bar and milk. He passed gas, multiple times,

I finally said, "QUIT THAT". He said, "It's okay now, I'm all out of air."

Then as we were pulling out of the driveway he says, "Hey Mom, let's get this party started". Ooh, who knew going to work, daycare and Papaw Ed's could constitute

as getting a party started but hey, I like his enthusiasm and am reminded I should view every day that God gives with JOY and it's HIS party, and another day to enjoy his blessings. God is talking through this sweet child of mine.

Just when I think he can't come up with ANY more that morning, I again am pleasantly surprised. I am talking to my friend, and Beau's little intuitive ears are listening.

We were conversating about a potentially bad situation that turned out well. I said to her very thankfully, "Oh thank God! How frightening!" Beau, only hearing bits and pieces of this adult conversation about life says, "Don't call me God, I'm not God, I'm Beau Rafferty". Paul and I can only pray his opinion of himself changes when he becomes a teenager. But for now, were safe, and I am thankful Mary was chosen to mother God in the flesh and not me!

One Friday evening Brynna had convinced me she felt ready to get her ears pierced...I have to admit I was a little reluctant and I am not sure why. I call Paul and we discuss the prospect of the ear piercing. He asks me where was I thinking of taking her. I told that one of our friends had taken her daughter to a ear-piercing kiosk in the mall and that the staff was really good with girls her age. He gives me his blessing, and we are off to the mall!

On the way, I didn't hide the fact that it may be a little painful. I could see immediately she didn't seem to mind.

We arrive to the mall and make our way to the kiosk. There is now wait. My little lady hops up in the "piercing chair", she really takes to the woman about to pierce her ears and possibly inflict pain on her. She tells the woman that she just called her Memaw Debbie and told her she was getting her ears pierced. The woman asked if Mom was coming, Brynna quickly unloads a conversation on this poor unassuming woman, "No my Memaw Debbie and Papaw Terry live in Hartford, Papaw Irnin lives in Beaver Dam, Papaw Terry calls it Beaver Cuss, but I know better. Well Papaw Irnin lives in Heaven now with my Mammaw Evelyn and Memaw and Papaw's dog Macy with Jesus." Brynna stops for air. The woman was laughing hysterically, and then Brynna says, "Are you going to pierce my ears now?" The woman was just waiting for her to be quiet. Apparently, she has just like her MOTHER, or so I've heard.

The piercing finally commences with relatively no reaction from Brynna at all.

Brynn decides to unload a little more on her by saying, "One time, when I was four I got two shots, one in my left shoulder and one in my right shoulder. I just said 'ouch', it didn't really hurt and I got two cool Bugs Bunny band aids, one for this arm and one for this arm."

By the time we finished me and Kathy (the ear piercing woman) were on a first name basis because my little social butterfly had all but invited her to our next family reunion! So, if you have a meeting or party and need an icebreaker, I am thinking about renting Brynna out for those of you who are interested. I can't promise that she won't go over her "allotted time", if you know what I'm saying. The girl can talk!

It was a Wednesday, and I was in the bed most of the evening with pain (doctor says most likely my arthritis). That evening I ate supper and a snack in bed. Brynn about four at this time came in wanting to know what kind of snack I was eating. My friend Holly had told me that she had bought the some chocolate fiber bars and that she gives them to her kids saying they were candy bars. I myself had been eating them for sometime myself but never thought to try it out on the kids. I thought Holly was really onto something here. Surely, they haven't discovered that the word "fiber" is an enemy to them yet. Plus, if you ask me, they are as good as a candy bar, so that is what I tell her, "It's a candy bar. You want one?" I am thinking she gets her snack and fiber, CHA-CHING!

I get her the bar and am trying to act coy. That was so hard, because I am having a party in my head over this little victory of getting Ms. Thing to eat a fiber bar. She is sitting in the recliner in our bedroom with her feet in the seat b/c she is so small the chair swallows her. She starts eating and says, "Mom this candy bar is GREAT, I love it". I tell her that was good to hear and just keep eating it. So she does until it is ALL GONE! I was beaming on the inside because she is like her brother, won't eat hardly anything but what she likes. She then says with the cutest smile, "Mom my belly is telling me it wants ANOTHER candy bar". I said, "Oh it is, well I think that's enough". I am really concerned with a fiber overload to be honest because they are PACKED with fiber. She then says, "Mom, do you hear that, it's my belly and it's saying it REALLY wants another candy bar". I said, "It is?" She then says with the straightest face, "Yeah don't you hear it? It's not a FART, I promise, it just wants more".

Boy was I glad it wasn't a fart but I couldn't promise tomorrow wasn't going to be full of them after the 9 grams of fiber her little belly had ingested.

It really seemed like any other day, the afternoon went smooth and I was hoping the evening would also be uneventful. I arrived to pick up Brynn and Beau from after school and both kids didn't notice me right away. Once Brynn laid her eyes on me she smiled and ran up to me but not so much with anticipation but with more of an "I think I am going to be in trouble" look on her face. To my dismay she tells me she got a card turned in her class, the card turn was a consequence because she hadn't followed directions. I chose not to address it at that moment because there was a room full of children that didn't deserve to see my wrath on her, that and I didn't want to embarrass her.

We get home and she sat on the floor as I sat on the ottoman in our living room. Paul is now with us and is laying on one of our couches. I began to tell Paul about the events of the day, as I knew them. At this point, she just listened as I told her Father of the "turning of the card". She had yet to own up to any wrong doing. We begin interrogating her, that sounds harsh but I am sure in her kindergarten mind that is exactly how she saw it. We ask her why she got the card turned and she begins to explain with a very colorful story that she had touched someone who said, "Don't touch me again" and that the card was turned for touching her neighbor. She had this peculiar look on her face so I felt like I had no other choice but ask her again what happened. This time she says, "I wasn't following directions?" She posed it as a question. I thought to myself, "I don't know I am the one asking you. Were you following directions?" At this point, Paul and I are so confused about what even happened we don't know which way is up or down.

We are at our boiling point and really just want to know what happened. Unfortunately, we had been over a course of action if she were to get a card turned that week due to an incident the week before. Her Dad, with authority, asks her, "What did I say would happen if you got a card turned this week?" She very confidently says (though teary-eyed), "That I wouldn't get an ipod". I was like, "WHAT IN THE WORLD??!!"...people she wasn't, at that point, getting an ipod anyway, so that was obviously not the punishment or repercussion for her bad behavior. Keep in mind; Paul and I both were holding back the laughter. She then goes into this dramatic monologue of "my brain hurts, I can't remember what happened, and this is so hard on me". I no longer watch soap operas but I was almost convinced she had amnesia and didn't have clear recollection of the previous conversation or perhaps this was her evil twin, we were dealing with. At this point, we are almost crying too because we are holding back our laughter. When finally it happened, not necessarily the response we were expecting. "Okay, okay...I got TWO cards turned". We aren't laughing anymore at this point...TWO CARDS???

I then wise up and think to myself...did she tell us the truth about touching someone? So I say, "did you get your cards turned because you were touching someone or did something else happen?" At this question, she fesses up and the bout with amnesia is over, "Okay, okay it was something else that happened", but she could never quite get out the whole story. So, it seemed we had only one recourse, the dreaded call to the teacher!! I didn't so much dread it, as Brynna did. Paul and I were now really curious about how the events of the day went down. After seeing that I was seriously placing a call, she threw her hands up in the air and ran into the family room screaming, "You can't call Ms. Lewis because that will ruin everything!" The drama was straight out of an Academy Award winning movie... it was impressive. What were we going to ruin? Was it her reputation with the teacher? I think she sealed that one up pretty good herself!

I get in touch with the teacher and to my not-so-much-surprise Brynn was in trouble for two different things... first for playing Mommy to all the kids...bossing them around in the restroom telling who to go to what stall...and how to properly wash their hands after being told to mind her business. And then...don't be SHOCKED please...for TALKING TOO MUCH! Where in the world would this child get this from?? Someone please tell me!

So, I ask of all my fellow parents, especially of older children...tell me it gets better and that these issues will never come up again. You can't tell me that, can you? I knew it. It makes for good fodder and at least now, we are more prepared. That taught us a good lesson, always have your child's teacher on speed dial and don't be afraid to use it!

Deliver Us and Our Children

As you have seen through the text of this book it looks as though I have used humor as my only defense. WRONG! I would never want it to appear that way. It would have been so easy for me to have gotten mad (which Paul and I did) at Brynn when the cards got turned at school, however I am thankful he also allows me to see the funny things...like the drama from our girl. I view it that God has given me, yet another tool, through His word, to combat the enemy. Laughter is one of the many defenses God has shown me. Read the below verse from Psalms.

Psalm 31:14-15 (NIV)

But I trust in you, O LORD; I say, 'You are my God.' My times are in your hands; deliver me from my enemies and from those who pursue me."

I think that is pretty powerful. It speaks to me telling me, I don't have the "power" to deliver myself from when my enemies pursue me or attack me, if you will. However, when I trust in the Lord and my life is in His hands, I can ask him to deliver me from my enemies. Sometimes I ask things very selfishly of God. Please take "this" away and "that" away, when perhaps I should be saying, "Lord, I put my trust in you and through that trust please deliver me". I am thankful He has delivered me, from many things and because I have seen His grace at work, I want to trust Him even more.

Though I look to the Word for my own deliverance, perhaps I should be more in communion with God when it comes to the deliverance of my children in situations when I am dumbfounded by what they say. 'Cause this one, caught me completely off guard. As I'm minding my own business in the kitchen one evening Brynn comes up to me as I am cooking dinner and says, "Mom, I really want to be a devil next Halloween" I said, "What? Why?" She says, "Yeah, with a tail and every thing. My friend Delaney is going to be one". I told her "NO!" she said, "But I will be a nice one, not like Lucifer was mean to Jesus". We took the kids to see a play in the Smokey Mountains on a family vacation and we saw a beautiful play on the life of Jesus. The only thing not biblical in the play seemed to be the use of making Lucifer a part of the plot during Jesus' life. They actually had a Good vs. Evil battle. Jesus WON! Anyway, I started rolling (my MAIN defense these days with my kids). She apparently didn't think what she said was funny and then says, "Mom, I am tired of being princesses". Let me set this straight, that year; she was the yellow female power ranger for Halloween, not a princess.

In the same weekend her devilish tendencies reared again, she begins telling singing to me, "We Will Rock You", but it's not the classic Queen version...there is something about a volcano...and shaking you up...and some other jargon that I don't know or couldn't understand. Just as she is about to finish the song it's rhyming and so help me I thought she was going to say the cuss word for butt...and she then says very cleverly in its place "EVERYBODY"...because that is how the song goes. Trying to make the listener think you are going to cuss, just to insert a cheery "EVERYBODY". I asked her very concerned, "Did you hear that at school?" She says, "No, day camp". I said who taught you...she then says, "The 9 and ups". Paul and I can't muffle the laughter at the phrase "the 9 and ups", but my mind automatically went to "why in the world are the 9 and ups cavorting with the 8 and unders and singing such controversial lyrics". Note to self, speak day camp staff Monday morning.

Apparently, she was amped up that weekend. She comes into our room around bedtime and says, "Mom, I want to watch Bob the Builder goes to Mexico when I am falling asleep". I am thinking to myself, "Bob the Builder goes to Mexico? I don't remember that episode". I asked her where she had seen that. She said, "Beau's watching it in his room". I decide to mosey into his room to see the episode but I'm still thinking, "I still have NO CLUE what that one is about. Is there a Hispanic character I am not aware of?" I enter his room and low and behold, Beau is playing the Bob the Builder DVD in Spanish. I look at him and we both start laughing. I inquired about what he was doing and he says, "I wanted to hear Bob talk in Spanish, so I pressed Spanish". Brynn just as serious as she can be says, "See Mom, I told you, Bob the Builder goes to Mexico". We had the hardest time finding out how to switch it back to English; I guess he was ready to come back to America.

Soon after Bob the Builder goes to Mexico became a favorite among the kids. I was routinely cleaning out Beau's backpack when I come across the daily "smiley" sheet. This form was used to help Beau follow directions better in his resource time. It was very helpful because he really hated to lose smileys. But, I mean who wouldn't, right? Anyway, on this particular smiley sheet I notice there is a note at the bottom from his teacher. This is what it said:

"Jaime, I just wanted to tell you that you have a bilingual child now! Beau told me and Mr. Drew that he could speak Spanish AND Chinese. He demonstrated for us. It kind of sounded like R2D2 (Star Wars)".

As you can imagine by now, I couldn't wait to share the news of Beau's new languages with his Dad! Beau for a couple of weeks had been talking about Spanish, putting all the DVD's on Spanish mode now, those that had that option and also making up his own words that he deemed as Spanish. So I asked Beau (who at this point is sitting at the bar in the kitchen leaned over on his elbows watching me read the note) if he could speak Chinese and Spanish. He looked at me very confidently and without a flinch responded, "Si". For those of you not bilingual like our son, that means "yes".

I thought Brynna had learned her lesson, as it related to behaving at school, I really did, but who am I kidding? We as adults mess up so many times and still need divine intervention to right our wrongs. Brynn went several months without a card being turned at school, or even so much as a warning. This was such a blessing to us. Though trying to be optimistic, I was afraid our luck would run out and a few months later, it did. It was an afternoon in May and my turn to pick up the two little hoodlums (one hoodlum: Brynna and a potential troublemaker: Beau) from after-school. As Brynn walks towards me, I know its bad news, I was born at night, but it wasn't last night and I recognized that "look". She grabs my upper leg as she reaches me and with very sad eyes says, "I turned a card today." I was exasperated and walking out the door I said, "Brynna Layne!" We get outside and I say, "Let me guess, you were talking?" She says, "The first time." I said, "THE FIRST TIME?!" This obviously implies another time! So I stop, kneel in front of her and make her look me in the eyes to tell me what happened. She says through the tears, "I was talking to my neighbor…" and doesn't tell me what happened the second time, so I say, "AND????" She puts her hands up to my ears and whispers, "I <u>might</u> have been galloping like a pony around the classroom". I said, "You might?? Why in the world were you doing that?" Perhaps she was inspired by the Kentucky Derby, which we had watched the Saturday prior…who knows! She says, in great Brynna DRAMA throwing her hands down and crying uncontrollably, "It seemed like a good idea!" I told her I don't know what part of it seemed like a good idea. Anyway, we are on our way home and she asks if I am going to "tell her father??" I tell her YES. She then is sort of somber and then with some conviction says, "Well I haven't turned TWO cards since September??" This kid has a mind like a steel trap…I had to stop and think myself…and she was right, it was the night I actually had to place the "CALL" to Ms. Lewis and get the "real" story because the "Brynna version" was a wee bit hazy! I told her anytime she turns a card it's NOT good! However she did win the classroom derby, I am sure that was a great honor among her peers.

The Wonder of God

I am not good at handling stress, that's what I like to write "funny" things down, it's therapeutic for me and it helps me realize life is too short to be miserable or to make other's miserable. You know the kind I am talking about? Have you ever had a day when you were just "up to here" with someone's antics? Maybe it was at home, school, work... wherever!

Apparently, it was "that kind of day" for Beau and he hadn't even gone to school yet. His little sister, who he usually adores, woke up on the wrong side of the bed. She was not a happy camper, about anything. If she complained once about something, she complained a million times (embellishing gives me no sympathy, does it?). Mind you, I woke her up at 6:50, and we leave at 7:15 so she squeezed in A LOT of complaining in a very short amount of time.

About 7:10 I am flat ironing my hair and Beau comes in my bathroom acting like he is hiding, burying his sweet face in my shirt/stomach. For those of you that REALLY know Beau, he is frequently very happy and bluntly honest (when he talks) because he is a very rigid thinker, which for some fun conversations! I asked him what he was doing, he said very seriously sounding put out, "I'm hiding from Brynny. I want to hide from my sister". I asked him "why"...he gave no response. He then said, "Don't yell for her!"... I said "why?" he said, "I DON'T WANT TO SEE HER"...again I said "why?"...and that's when the statement of TRUTH came out, "I don't want to see her cause she is SUCH a whiner". I laughed and he said very seriously, "Why is she a whiner??" To which I responded very honestly, "Don't I wish I knew!" Autism really isn't so bad, is it? At least Beau can speak with honesty and not get in trouble! If you find out why Brynna is such a whiner, could you let Beau know? While you're on the case, just let me and Paul know too. That'd be great as it would answer an ages old (only about seven years really) question for us. Thanks!

One average weekday, I went to pick the kids up from school. Upon entering the building, I happen upon one of Brynna's teachers. She says to me without even taking a breath, "Hey are you guys going to a new church? I heard you crashed your car AGAIN. Did you guys get a Nintendo Wii? How about Nintendo DS's, did the kids them too? Did they take the DS's to their grandparents' house over the weekend?" She said even more than that, but I will stop there. I asked her to slow down just so I could process all the questions she posed. I also was thinking, "How she could possibly know so much about us". She then said laughing, "Don't tell YOUR DAUGHTER anything you don't want told because she tells me EVERYTHING about you guys". My face was probably five lovely shades of red, it felt very red! I am not sure if Brynna was recording us incognito or if she has a memory and possibly mouth like her Mommy's (I'm going for the latter). Yep, it's going to be pretty quiet around the Rafferty house in the near future! Actually, we started that night.

You might want to keep record of what I am about to say. For those of you that might encounter my sweet little girl sometime in your life, if you don't want it repeated, don't tell Brynna! Or, just tell us yourselves and save her the trouble (of getting in trouble).

I was driving the kids to school, we were on a one-hour weather delay but the "Mom express" was early. Before taking them to school, I scoot into Panera to get some of their divine hazelnut coffee. As I pull away Brynn says too me "When we go home today Mom, I am going to get my piggy bank and turn it upside down and bang on it"...I said, "Why?"...she says, "To get some money out"...I say, "For who?" Very seriously, she says, "For you Mom!" I then said again, "Why?" She says, "Cause your always telling Daddy (as she changes her voice to sound somewhat like mine) 'Don't eat out anymore this week Paul, we don't have any money!' that's why!". She apparently took that exaggerated statement of mine very seriously. Next thing I know she will be having a telethon for her Mommy and Daddy raising, eating out money for him and coffee money for me. Bless her heart she knows where our priorities are.

You know some things you just can't make up!! This is one of them! ;)

I know we often see the wonder of God in our children. I saw it in Beau...yet again. I see it often (in both he and Brynn), but the innocence I saw on this particular occasion blessed me in an extra special way.

It was wacky hair day at the YMCA. When we got to day camp, Beau told me to mess up his hair. We keep his hair very short and because of the buzz cut there really isn't much I can do. So, to pacify him, I just took my hand and rubbed it across it back and forth really quickly until he asked me politely to stop. He said, "There Mom, now that's perfect". As you can imagine, it looked exactly the same, but I just smile, inside and out.

He continued eating his McDonald's hash brown but now he smiling from ear to ear because he had "wacky hair". Beau wanted it because it was "wacky hair day" and he likes the structure of following directions (sometimes...LOL!!), not because he cared about looking like everyone else. Oh to be more like that!! He thanked me before I left. I really think when it comes to Beau, we are entertaining angels unaware...or maybe we are aware now. His innocence and perspective is something that can't be duplicated and can only be from God.

I think about that a lot, looking like everyone else. We, as human beings like to think we are our own people, just to go and replicate some actress' hair or clothing style. I am as guilty as the next person. I remember saying I would NEVER wear skinny jeans, fearing I would look like a sugar cone. Then one day when I was browsing American Eagle, one of their lovely clerks brainwashed me into trying a pair on. Then to make matters worse, I loved them, I wanted to buy a pair in every color (I have tendencies to do that with things I love...shoes, jeans, purses...you get the drift). Unfortunately they only came in a dark wash, and I got one pair. Then there was the "boot craze", which at the time I am writing this is still going on. The "slouchy" boots with the skinny jeans tucked in. Another trend I swore I would never do again, thanks do in part to a bad memory from middle school. What happens, I did it again...bought more skinny jeans and more boots to tuck the jeans in. I have a friend who tells me to call her every time I feel the need to go shopping. I guess you can see I haven't called her nearly as much as I should have.

Let me get to the point, there was a point in all the ranting. With Beau, right now in his life, he just sees himself like everyone else. Isn't that beautiful?? He puts no additional effort into trying to fit in. One evening he actually put on a cape, a pair of sunglasses that were $$ over the eyes, socks on his hands and underwear on his head and thought that was a grand ensemble to parade around in. I give God glory for this, well not necessarily the underwear on his head, but that he doesn't seem to mind about appearances. Paul and I will be blessed for as long as this lasts! I pray he never sees himself as "different" in a way that causes separation, but embraces that God made him uniquely with a specific purpose in mind, HIS PLAN and HIS PURPOSE! We sometimes separate ourselves or become separated from friends because we don't fit in with them anymore, family because they don't accept us for choices we have made…and I could go on forever there. So with all the heartache autism could bring, it doesn't bring us heartache in that area…at least not for now. It brings us yet another much needed life lesson.

Our Funny Kids

I don't know what it is about this part of the country but I am most of the people I know suffer from sinus and allergy afflictions. It seems that once I reached adulthood they emerged. One day in particular I was feeling especially down and out in my sinus cavity. Luckily, because of inclement weather I was also off of work. This day I was lazy and decided to lie in the bed with both babies (they were both school-aged but they are still our babies!) beside me. It doesn't take long in that given scenario for me to doze off, and I did. I am not sure how long I had been out, when I suddenly feel these little arms wrap around me, one behind my head and the other around my waist, and eye open my eyes a bit startled and Beau plants a big one on me and says, "Man, that was a good kiss!". I thought I was going to lose it! Who know a kid could get so much enjoyment out of kissing his old mommy?! Talk about the medicine I needed, I think that was just what the doctor had ordered that day. These are the days of our lives!

I just wanted you to know...in case you have posted flyers about your community...Beau announced very loudly and proudly one evening, as Paul and I were having a meaningful conversation..."I FOUND NEMO". So if you, or anyone else is looking for him he is no longer lost, apparently he is at my house...in Beau's room. Mystery solved!

Who can't get enough of Brynna?? Oooohhhh ME!! :)

It was spring and nearing the last day school. Summer break was on the horizon and the kids could not wait. Before the year came to a close the kid's school was having their annual field day. Beau didn't really express any interest in it, but Brynna could hardly contain herself. She was telling me how excited she was about it. I told her when I was little, (she always says, "In your town?") our school also had field day. She strays from her field day for a moment and begins her own monologue about how we don't live there but she thinks it looks like it would have been a "nice" place to grow up. Somewhere in the conversation I here her say, though she likes to visit her Memaw and Papaw there, it has "dirty buildings but it's still kind of pretty" (God bless the mayor, should this ever cross their path).

After the digression and side bar about where I grew up she returns to the thought of field day and me saying I had field day in grade school. She looks at me scrunches up that cute face and says, "really, you had a field day...at your school?" I told her yes and that I loved it because we would have 3-legged races, potato sack races and wheelbarrow races! Though I never won any of the above, I didn't let my lack of athletic ability squelch my enthusiasm. She told me I had field day all wrong, all they were going to do was play in a field all day out behind the school. I was, overcome with laughter. She didn't find it funny at all and she flat argued with me about the events of field day. Are you surprised?

We arrive at the school and they are setting up inflatables on the school lawn...she says in utter disgust and disbelief, "I thought this was supposed to be field day, that is NOT a field, it's the front of the school and the parking lot". I just smiled...my girl is so literal. If I were her, I would be ecstatic that I wouldn't have to play in a field all day...but what do I know, I'm just from Kentucky.

Beau spent an entire weekend with my Mom and Dad. Lord only knows what kind of expressions my comical Father used in his presence (sorry Dad...but you know it's true!). I'm going to assume my Dad might have said this to Beau over the weekend...he's known to move at two paces... slow and STOP.

After my parents brought the kids home from their weekend visit we decided to take them to Cracker Barrel for supper. In case I haven't driven the point home, Beau is a very rigid thinker and speaks his mind even when sometimes it may sound a bit rude. Some may say this is just him being a boy/male, but I disagree, I have met many men that don't always speak their mind…and actually more women that I wish wouldn't. However, in this instant Beau had something to say and apparently he thought the service took far too long. Paul and I hadn't really noticed the time lapse as Beau did. He looked at Paul and me and said, "Where's our food?" We told him to be patient and it would be arrive in a minute. He said just as serious as he could..."Would someone get back there and tell them to quit lolly-gagging".

They must have heard him, after that, our food came right up! He's going to every restaurant with me now… especially the drive thru windows.

Brynna asked me something pretty funny one night... that really came out of left field! Well it wasn't THAT funny, but I had to laugh (because as many people know, that's what I do).

She has a million stuffed animals, okay maybe not a million, but I would guesstimate about fifty cuddly friends. Barbies and dolls aren't or have never been her thing... stuffed animals are. I was just the opposite, hated stuffed animals...loved me some dolls. I often joke, if it were socially acceptable I would still play with Barbies. Anyway, I was handing her one of her bears (she has named them ALL) and I said, "Here's Beary." She very proudly says, "Don't you know that's not Beary, he's over there, that's Icy"...duh Jaime can't you keep them straight...and I go to hand her another one she got for her birthday that year and I say, here's this one (not knowing it's name) and she says, "Oh that's Emily". Mind you, about 50% of her animals have the name Emily. So I said, "Why don't you name it something else". She asked me for some ideas (she likes real names for some of them obviously). I told her that at one time, Daddy and I had thought about having another baby and naming her Rebekah if it was a girl and calling her Bekah and that I like that name for one of her animals. She then said, "You know, you really should have had another baby". I told her it wasn't in our "plan from God". She said, "How do you get a baby". I told her you go to the hospital without a baby, and you come home with a baby. I thought that was a GREAT answer. My little genius then says, "NO MOM, how do you make a baby?" I FROZE....started blushing...giggling and just dying inside. I told her the only logical thing I could think of to tell a 6 year-old. "Mommy and Daddy work with God for 9 months to make this baby together and that's why the belly grows, because a baby can't come into the world if it's not ready". I just tried to focus on the "growth" of the baby and not the making of it. I sure hope it's a long time before she asks any more questions like that. We'll have to wait and see how long that answer holds out!

Lighten Up

Brynna and I decided on this very special Father's Day we would wake up early and give Paul his cards from all of us. Brynn says, "Mom, where's that secret present I made for Dad for Father's Day?" I am thinking to myself, what "secret present" is she talking about? Then it dawns on me, before school let out they made a Father's Day gift and she told me to put it away in a safe place. So, I did. I bet it's really safe now, because I couldn't find his present ANYWHERE and I looked ALL over. Don't you love it when you do that? Hide something so someone else won't find it, and you really just end up hiding it from yourself? So, as I am fumbling through one of my "junk cabinets" (yes that is plural because I do have more than one) looking for it. However, this present was not junk, but it may have unintentionally landed there by accident of course. In the process of searching our typical hiding places, she sees this sheep made of construction paper and cotton balls she made in Sunday school about two months prior and says...and I quote, "Aaaahhh, here just give me that, he liked it the first time, I bet he'll like it again". That's right, Brynna just "re-gifted" an arts and crafts project, and on Father's Day no less! I CERTAINLY didn't teach her that but I had to hand it too her for thinking on her feet. Anyway, she hands him the cotton ball sheep and says, "Here I couldn't find your real present, and do you like this old one? Happy Father's Day Daddy!"

Paul said the "gift" really made his day special, I am sure that was true because you couldn't replicate a laugh like that!

Beau is known for having some rough mornings. He doesn't sleep well at night. Sometimes staying up long after his television has been turned off and the lights are out. One morning in particular was indeed a rough morning. He's a Sponge Bob fan so I nicknamed him Beau Bob Cranky Pants. In light of tantrum, Paul and I had to have a talk with him that evening about his attitude when getting dressed and ready to leave the house each morning. He listened pretty intently and was a joy the rest of that evening. I even got a great hug and kiss out of it from Mr. Cranky Pants, himself. Paul and I nominated ourselves for Parents of the Year after that intervention.

The next morning he arises (I am in the kitchen) and he announces very proudly, "I am so happy, it's going to be a GREAT day". I almost begin laughing aloud. I suppose to the average person this sounds very condescending after the previous morning's events, right? Well Beau really meant it and I quickly find out that he is in RARE form!

He is sitting in our room watching one his favorite morning shows called Martha Speaks. It's a very cute and educational show about a dog that has eaten alphabet soup. The consumption of the soup gave her the ability to speak. Beau is quite intrigued, by this talking dog and tells me that he wants to meet Martha. I tell him that she is a cartoon so he can't. He then says, "I can go see her in the TV". NOPE! Then he asks me why our cats, Job and Scoots don't talk.

This was getting far too deep at 6:30am for me. He asks if I will buy them some alphabet soup to eat...NOPE! Then he asks if we can buy a talking cat... and again I say NOPE! I'm already feeling a bit like Beau felt the morning before, Mom-Bob Cranky Pants.

Finally, we get out of the house, after Beau has realized he will never have a talking animal. I am at our normal intersection to turn on the main thoroughfare and the stop light...will NOT turn. I kid you not we sat there through 3-4 light turns for the North and South Lanes. The kids were getting antsy, as was already in antsy pants mode. I was a more in a rush because I had major work project I needed to complete. As I sit there and contemplate all I need to accomplish that day, I hear Beau say, "Hi, Hi". I can see, out of my peripheral vision that he is waving. I look over my right should and see a man, and what looks to be his son waving and smiling. Beau is sort of hollering, "Look at me Mom, I like to wave to 'nice' strangers. Oh, look...look the nice strangers are waving and smiling back at me. This is good, this is good." I am not sure how to differentiate for certain, nice strangers from not-so-nice strangers but apparently, Beau can. After six LONG minutes, the light finally turns and we are on our way to the YMCA. Yes, I watched the clock, and I even contemplated calling 911. It would have been more of a warning about a maniacal Mommy in a family car who was about to ram into something if the light didn't turn. I'm saddened to admit this Mommy; she looked a whole lot like me. Thank goodness for K-Love Christian radio and it's calming and soothing effect on me during times of duress.

When we get to the YMCA Brynn jumps right out of the car. And Beau, well I don't really know what Beau was doing. Some days, as we have established, he has the two speeds of slow and stop. This day he was rotating them both equally. I am already worked up and trying to get him moving. I said, "C'mon Beau we need to GO, Mommy's going to be late to work". He piddles around and finally gets out of the car...stops (again) dead in his tracks...puts his hands on his hips, looks at me and says, "Mom, you need to lighten up". Because you know, he's always easy, easy like Sunday morning...WHATEVER. He had given me an award-winning tantrum just the previous morning. Mind you, I will use this very phrase on him on those mornings he throwing a fit because he doesn't like his Transformer flip-flops or his "adult" shoes as he calls them (because he actually has to tie them unassisted). Again, I think this is from the arsenal of my Dad...but I can't be certain.

So the moral of this story is...don't get in a hurry...and if you do...LIGHTEN UP!

I struggle with this whole "lighten up" mentality. I really do. I try to present myself as happy-go-lucky and for the most part I am. But, I can get my knickers in a twist pretty quickly. I don't like many drivers on the road, and I am guilty of road rage, almost every time I get behind the wheel. I also have many days where I don't like autism…at all. It's not so much that I get mad at God, I get frustrated with the limitations it puts on Beau's abilities. However, Beau has no clue he has limitations. Momma's the one not seeing the blessing that day. Recently as Paul and I were reading our devotion God spoke to me about why I get my vision skewed.

Hebrews 12:1-3 (New International Version)

[1]Therefore, since we are surrounded by such a great cloud of witnesses, let us throw off everything that hinders and the sin that so easily entangles, and let us run with perseverance the race marked out for us. [2]Let us fix our eyes on Jesus, the author and

perfecter of our faith, who for the joy set before him endured the cross, scorning its shame, and sat down at the right hand of the throne of God. ³Consider him who endured such opposition from sinful men, so that you will not grow weary and lose heart.

WOW, when I read that, and then read it again (I knew God was speaking to ME specifically on this one)...and we "fix our eyes on Jesus" all those things of the world that hinder us have already been overcome by Him and He can help us persevere through them too! I also think about what he went through for me, for you, for all of us. It gives me chills to see the words "joy" with "the cross". I don't know about you, but as I watch recreations of the crucifixion it can no way touch the true horror that many people witnessed that day, but the bottom line was he saw the "joy" in the process of what was being done through Him on the cross. There was an end result that was worth it. He endured much more than I will ever have too. Kind of makes that slow driver seem like no inconvenience at all, and autism just speed bump in the road of life. I am very encouraged not to grow weary or lose heart. He kept his eyes fixed on the end result. I am called to do the same...even when I want to lay down and through an award winning tantrum right beside Beau. I must remind myself to fix my eyes on Jesus every day.

I don't like to be mad or uptight. That's why I have to seek God's help. I am finding how much I enjoy seeing the humor, through His hand, in the funny things of life. This next story is no different. One morning as the kids and I are backing out of the driveway, I realize I must have left my University of Louisville coffee travel mug filled with the delicious coffee Paul made in the house. I am still in my neighborhood when I turn the car around to head back to the homestead. It dawns on me that it actually may be on top of my car. I am the proverbial chicken running around with its head cut off. I say aloud, "I think it's on the car". Brynna begins SCREAMING at the top of her lungs, "OH MY GOSH, OH MY GOSH there is a cup of hot coffee on top of our car. Get it Mom, get it!" Beau is looking at her like she is insane with his ears plugged. I am like, "WHY ARE YOU SCREAMING??? I THINK it's there, it's not going to hurt anything." She just keeps going, "Aaahhh, aaahhh, aaahhh". I pull in our driveway, mind you, she is STILL screaming...and there it is, sitting peacefully on top of the car. I pulled the cup down and just laughed at her reaction. I turn around and showed her the cup was "closed" and thought to myself that we were lucky it didn't spill on the car (because Paul had just washed it). I said, "See it turned out just fine". She smiles, gives a fist pump in the air and says, "Go Cards!" As if to say, it was the Cardinal power that kept the hot coffee from spilling...Paul and I have taught her right...a girl after our own hearts! Go Brynn and GO CARDS!

Go Cards...But Watch Your Step!

It was my typical Tuesday lunch hour and I needed to do a little shopping, well I wanted to do a little shopping, sometimes I have a trouble differentiating needs and wants. This time I wanted to go shopping, I am pretty sure of it. The day was really yucky outside, raining just enough to annoy you and to have to use your windshield wipers. After a brief bout of shopping, I am feeling like I NEED some coffee to beat the afternoon blahs! I am a person, who could drink coffee morning, noon and night. I walk over to Target where there is a Starbucks kiosk located conveniently inside. I know what I am getting before I even reach the counter. This afternoon is calling for a Pike Place blend with a shot of sugar free caramel for good measure. I am doing great at this point...not even caring it's raining. I am wearing a jean skirt, flip-flops and a casual shirt (this will play a small roll in the fiasco momentarily). As I am walking out of the store, I hear a married couple I went to high school with say "hello". I politely say "hello" and go on outside with my sturdy University of Louisville umbrella. I am thinking back on the couple...oh I haven't seen them in forever, they are so sweet...stuff like that. I get outside and as I walk into the cross walk, I am not paying any attention to my footing, and why should I; I have the fluid movements of a ballerina (everyone that knows me is now laughing their heads off). My once cute flip-flop (has now become my worst enemy) slides on the slippery yellow paint. By this time, it's raining like a typhoon and my jean-skirt clad butt goes down like the Titanic. Mind you, all the while I am holding a piping hot cup of Joe...that I don't even spill...now that's talent. I hear this woman YELL (I'm praying NO ONE saw me), "Oh goodness honey, oh goodness...are you okay?" I want to say... shut up woman (as she is drawing more attention to me, the klutz on the ground)...I jump RIGHT UP...FAST...as I begin to walk away...the pain sets in and I mean quickly (I even begin moaning thinking why do I always parks SO far away...exercise seemed meaningless today!)...I have never been more thankful for the toosh warmers in the car. I also begin to process my priorities. I reflect on the fall and my desire to protect my coffee over my fragile body. That can't be natural but sometimes you do what you have to do!

I shake my head knowing once Paul hears about this one; he will not be surprised in the least. I am so glad my parents named me Jaime, and not Grace. With my tendencies to fall, walk into walls and have car accidents Grace carries way to much pressure.

Moral of the story...just because the flip-flops look cute and comfortable they are walking water hazard...or maybe I am the walking water hazard! WATCH YOUR STEP.

One morning I took Brynn and Beau to McDonalds to get them a breakfast sandwich. Brynn gets her usual sausage biscuit, and notices there is a picture on her sandwich. She asks me what it was. It was a little advertisement for the new McCafe coffees. I hear her in the back seat reading it..."Start your day with a mo-cha...Mom, what's a mo-cha?" I'm like, "honey I know it looks like it should make the CH sound like Cha-cha...but it's like a K sound, like mo-ka". She says, "Well, I don't know why they didn't just spell it m-o-k-a... McDonald's is stupid".

I couldn't disagree more with Brynna, just for the record. It's funny she didn't think the yummy sausage and biscuit she was eating was too "stupid". I got to thinking; McDonald's is at least a billion dollars smarter and richer than I am. So to the McDonald's corporation, my daughter is in grade school, I don't pay much attention to what she says, you probably shouldn't either!

The Singing Southern Installer

We were blessed to be able to get new doors in the summer of 2009. I arranged to take off work to meet the installer. So the afternoon started out great. I took before and after pictures of our house pre and post door. We had been saving for this day; waiting and anticipating for 5.5 years! It's beautiful...the new doors. We are still really enjoying it... like two kids.

But as usual the day didn't go down without a hitch...I was the hitch. For those who know how "bright" I can be, you should enjoy really this. Greg, the installer, was a very nice guy; though now living in Kentucky was originally from Alabama. He had quirky sayings, only HE could pull off with the heavy southern accent like, "that door's as tight as a fat guy in a wet suit". He brought his own radio. So as I sat, in anticipation, watching a little HGTV he plugged into a local country station and sang a wide variety of hits. I haven't figured out which one I liked best, Toby Keith's, "I'm Not as Good as I Once Was" or Lee Greenwood's, "Proud to be an American"...regardless it was quite a show and those songs will never be the same after his rendition. I guess I should have but I didn't tip him because I didn't ask for singing with the installation.

Anyway, between installing the entry door (which was up) and the storm door I got a little antsy, and couldn't sit still. I felt like I was watching a pot boil. I wanted to get out there with my camera and snap a shot of just the door. So, I told him. He obliged. I hopped up, shut the door, then went outside to snap the picture and guess what genius girl did? He asked me, "Ma'am you didn't happen to grab those keys I just handed you and bring them outside with you, did you?" Of course not, I can barely walk and chew gum.

I had locked us BOTH out of the house. Thank goodness, the "Singing Southern Installer" had a good sense of humor. He laughed and said he accustomed to being supervised by a woman. I was in no way trying to supervise I assure you of that, I was just being nosey. He says, "Don't worry Mrs. Rafferty, I'll just get my ladder and put the storm door on, if you'll call your husband and see if he can let us in". Good idea! So, I call Paul and hope he isn't too upset. He didn't think it was as funny as me and the installer, but thankfully he wasn't mad! Greg looks around for the ladder and guess what? He had taken it in the house right before Einstein (AKA me) locked the door. So he improvised and pulled his toolbox over to the door and used it as a ladder.

I then offered to take requests too sing. I was bored sitting on our brick planter mailbox outside the house there watching him hang a storm door. Apparently, he or none of the neighbors or anyone else wanted me to sing, imagine that. Paul arrives home, just in the knick of time, I was about to break out into "Praise You in This Storm" by Casting Crowns because that's all I could do…laugh at this situation. Once Paul lets us all in and he does laugh and in just a matter of minutes the installation is complete. Thankfully it was well before Greg's son's little league game, which he told Paul and I about. He never admitted it, but I think he was a wee bit panicked after the over-eager home owner locked him out of his job...go figure.

I think I have laid out pretty well for you how I get when I'm stressed, right? Well, if not, here is yet another example of my own genius tendencies hard at work. You have my permission to enjoy at my expense. I received an e-mail that was also sent to 25 other health care professionals; that requested prevention materials for a health care event.

I did have materials to spare and I sent this message to all 25 folks letting them know what my organization could provide to requesting agency:

"I have chopsticks with a breast cancer message (that also contain SPF). Would that work? If yes, am I understanding that you just need 12?"

I then get an e-mail from my good friend at the American Cancer Society asking me if I doing outreach, specifically to the Asian population. I went back, and re-read the e-mail and just shook my head in embarrassment. I obviously meant chapstick. A thought to ponder, spell check, friend or foe?

The Lord's Prayer

I'm guilty, really guilty of not stopping to pray for my shortcomings at the moment. I guess it's because I would be in a constant state of prayer. I may stop and pray for a friend in need, but when it comes to me and my reactive emotions I may think, "Naaah, I'm not going to bother God with this one, I think I've got it". Then after things fall apart because I have gone MY own way again, it dawns on me, "Girl, why didn't you take it too the Lord?" I know sometimes though, I am so emotional over the situation at hand; I just don't know what to pray, have you ever been like that?

Romans is helping guide me in this.

Romans 8:26-27 (New International Version)

[26]In the same way, the Spirit helps us in our weakness. We do not know what we ought to pray for, but the Spirit himself intercedes for us with groans that words cannot express. [27]And he who searches our hearts knows the mind of the Spirit, because the Spirit intercedes for the saints in accordance with God's will.

Man, that spoke to me saying that is why after Jesus was called up that the Holy Spirit is with us. I don't have to have the "right words". He knows my weakness and I can be in His presence with submitting to him that I need to pray, and he can search my heart and intercede for me. Beautiful! Isn't it funny how sometimes we think we have all the answers? Oh it's not "ha ha" funny, it's the irony that makes us think we "got this situation covered" and in times when we don't have the answers we go to him. I do this ALL THE TIME. However, he wants us in all things, the big and small things. Note to self, remember what you just said...he wants the big and small things...okay, got it!

Another tool I have used to help me, it may or may not be something you could use is the Lord's Prayer. I have a very sharp tongue. I remember being a kid and Matt and me getting into verbal arguments and me trying to find the meanest and ugliest words to pierce him. However, "butt head" just didn't hurt him like I had hoped it would. I am not a believer in the whole, "sticks and stones may break my bones but words will never hurt me". You know that is so untrue. I have had many bicycle accidents I cannot recall, however I can tell you when someone was mean to me in grade school and called me an ugly name. Now, I sit here wondering if I did that to someone and hurt their feelings and they are remembering it.

Apparently I never grew out of that retaliatory behavior. In some of my arguments as an adult I have done this very same thing. I am not proud of this, but I would still try to muster up words that would just cut like a knife because I was hurt and wanted the other person to feel the same pain I felt. Gosh that is an ugly trait, and I am embarrassed to even say that. As women, especially, we can be so mean to one another. Well, God convicted me of this. In times where I feel like I want to retaliate or say an ugly word and

I don't know what to pray, I pray the Lord's Prayer until my heart is right and I know longer want to say hurtful or ugly things. Now, forgive me if you hear me say this out loud in your presence, I guess I have just given my prayer tip away and perhaps I would like to call you a "butt head". In all seriousness, it is hard to want to call someone a bad name when you are reciting the prayer that was created to teach us how to pray. I don't just let it fly off my tongue either. I mentally repeat it, and have to force myself to feel the words I am saying. Does that even make sense? If not, try it the next time you get upset and maybe, just maybe you will understand what I mean. Or maybe you won't and you will just be gritting your teeth saying the Lord's Prayer.

One morning Brynn did one of the funniest things in my memory, well don't put much stock in that, I think everything is pretty funny. I dropped her and Beau off at the YMCA. She sits down on the floor by a little girl (who was about 8...Brynn is 6) who's eating her breakfast and has what looks like a Tiger Beat magazine with the Jonas Brothers and Miley Cyrus on the front. The little girl shows Brynna the magazine and says, "look it's the Jonas Bros, I call Joe...who do you call??" Brynn looks up at me sheepishly. I act as if I am not listening, because she gets embarrassed when I act like I am her mother, I have no clue why, I'm one of the coolest Mommy's I know and you are probably a cool Mom too. To make matters worse I sit down beside her just awaiting her answer...will it be Nick or Kevin, inquiring minds want to know. She starts pointing...but not at the magazine...in the air. I said, "What are you doing, what are you pointing at?"...she actually says to me..."THE DOOR!" I said, "Do you want me to leave"... before the words even leave my mouth she insists, "YES". I felt so unwanted. I knew at that point, it was the beginning of the end. As I sadly walked away, I could feel myself reciting the words to the every popular and so beautiful "Serenity Prayer". I wasn't mad so the Lord's Prayer went unsaid; however the Serenity Prayer provided me the same comfort.

Mammaw Evelyn Would Be Proud!

Move over Beau and Brynna...have Paul and I got a story for you?! It's fun to share stories of the kids, but I think I enjoy the funny things that happen to us as adults, just as much, maybe even a little more. Parts of this story may be a wee bit embellished for comedy's sake...but for the most party I would say it is at least 90% true! And Paul, I love you and was equally excited about the Oreck when you ordered it, I really was.

Paul has love and somewhat of an infatuation for infomercials. I guess the best case of this would be the Egg Genie, which we have used but at the most 3-4 times (in his defense I did take the initiative and actually order the thing). One night we stayed up later then normal and he felt compelled to watch QVC. Ironically, we had discussed the need to purchase a new vacuum cleaner earlier in the day. It seems that either we have too much dander and such to pick up or we are buy really low end vacuums...we have gone through 3 of them in less than 3 years. This is not something worth boasting, I assure you. He tells me this time we are not messing around with some namby-pamby vacuum. We will be getting either an Oreck or a Dyson.

Anyway, back to QVC (you know how I digress). I hear Paul say, "If I'm up at 11pm, I'm watching the Oreck challenge on QVC, I bet they will have vacuums on there. It's almost 11, I'll be up!" Was this a sign, or what? The first demonstration during the "Challenge" was for an air purifier. We definitely didn't want that...but Paul, I think, almost convinced himself (and me too) that it was a must have too. Luckily, it went unpurchased...thanks in large part to divine intervention...translation, me praying neither one of us would be THAT impressed! Then there it is the demonstration for the products of all products "THE VACUUM". This had been something that has been on Paul's wish list to purchase for the last 2-3 years. He and my Dad, Mom and I have had lengthy conversations about the Oreck and no, I am NOT kidding, we actually sat down and talked about vacuum cleaners and none of us even got bored. Before I know it, he's on the phone with QVC purchasing the RED Oreck at 6 E-Z payments of $$$/ month and we can't forget FREE shipping and handling (which I told Paul would kill us on a vacuum if we had to pay it…and it was FREE that night). I laid there in our bed, dozing in and out of consciousness...wondering if I heard what I thought I heard...Paul talking to the QVC people in the recliner next to the bed. Before I went to sleep I vaguely remember saying, "Mammaw Evelyn would be SO proud"... why, because she LOVED her some QVC too.

Well, it was true. First thing, the very next morning QVC sent me an e-mail confirmation of Paul's purchase, which was made at 11:30pm. They got him (and ME too!!) hook, line and vacuum cleaner! That shouldn't even be legal, you know that? Selling goods to people so late in the evening, when inhibitions are lowered and sleepiness is setting in. So we waited...I marked on my calendar August 24 and circled it...it would be the day the Oreck was to be delivered and hopefully changes our lives forever. I will keep you posted as the saga unfolds…because there's more.

It was undoubtedly Paul's "lucky day". First, the mail ran and Paul's long awaited University of Louisville season football tickets arrived. I texted him, just to let him know of the splendor that awaited him when he got home, and if he was having a bad day, that might help make it better. He wanted to know if the tickets looked "cool"…well of course… they are U of L football tickets! At U of L, apparently they think their ticket holders are uneducated as they number the tickets…1, 2, 3, 4, 5, 6…to let you know which ticket is for which of the 6 home games. How nice! As if, the date wasn't a dead giveaway!

Anyway, with that excitement aside, I laid back down in my bed. I had been out of commission due to a nasty bout of bronchitis. I heard the doorbell ring much to my chagrin. BUT, as I am approaching the door, I can see the UPS man driving away and I knew immediately what was waiting for me outside that door…THE ORECK…ready for its challenge! It had no idea exactly how much the Rafferty household, with all its dust and dander, would challenge that new Oreck.

I opened the door and brought it in the house…the QVC advertisement was so right, even boxed it weighed less than a gallon of milk. So far so good, there was no false advertising here. I text Paul again…it's like Christmas day at our house with the arrival of so many goodies in one afternoon. I didn't even attempt to put it together, as I knew Paul would relish this task. After an appointment that afternoon for Beau, we get home and Paul assembles the Oreck very quickly, further solidifying this purchase he had made near the stroke of Midnight one evening. He begins vacuuming…it was like a cult or something…he was just so drawn to the Oreck. I had never seen any human being, especially Paul, enjoy vacuuming so much in my life...further convincing me we really should have purchased this a LONG LONG time ago! The carpet never looked better...or maybe I didn't realize how BAD it looked until we got a vacuum that really sucks. It's so nice to use that word in a non-derogatory fashion. So, that was that. Paul kept saying, "Jaime, I think it even smells cleaner in here". Perhaps the vacuum had the special feature of being an air purifier too!

A while later Paul very convincingly tells me to vacuum our room. So...I grab the Oreck. It was like pushing a feather across the floor. Once I started...I couldn't stop... for real!! Paul was like, "I told you...you won't want to stop vacuuming". Oh my...he was so right, I think I could have vacuumed all night. I even wanted to take the thing next door to our neighbor's, the Gilmore's...and then to our other neighbor's the Brook's but that somehow seemed out of neighborly etiquette at 8:00pm, you know? Anyway, Paul basically, had to unplug it as my addiction set in, just to get me to stop...I was a lean mean vacuuming machine. You know...you too could be...if you would take the Oreck challenge. I mean, what's holding you back? Money? Pish-posh-hog-wash...6 E-Z payments! Need I say more?

The only thing the Oreck wouldn't do was change my carpet color...it's still teal...however, I can actually tell it's teal now...I guess that's a positive. Oh, how I love my "green" carpet. Not so much. All it needed was a "back nine" and it really would have been perfect, in Paul's eyes! So, all in all, the Oreck hasn't been a challenge at all, but a wonderful life-changing experience. It has been like chicken soup for the soul!

Insert Laughter Here

One Sunday after church, we had our ritualistic lunch at local haunt, Blair's Heartland Cafe...Paul, Me, Beau, Brynna and my father-in-law Ed. As we were leaving, we were discussing Brynn's athletic abilities and potential. She was playing soccer, and really showed great progress that season. Paul and I asked her if she wanted to play Upward Basketball too. She asked us if "girl's played", we told her yes, so she very enthusiastically agreed to consider it.

Paul announces that perhaps Santa would get her basketball goal. She says, "What if Santa's pilgrim's don't know how to make a basketball goal". A hush came over us...but as quickly as the hush came...so did the laughter from the three adults in the car. She starts SCREAMING in embarrassment, "I don't know what they're called; I don't know what they're called!!!" We all three went quiet...she was MAD! I said, "Do you mean elves, honey?" She said, "Yes". Ed says, "Brynna, the Pilgrims represent Thanksgiving". Trying to change the subject she says, "Yes, that's in November". Good girl! What kind of history are they teaching over at the elementary school, that's what I'd like to know?

She may not know that Pilgrims have NOTHING to do with making toys, but at least she knows which month Thanksgiving is! I apologize for even questioning the education that she is getting. As my friend, Lisa once told me, "God doesn't give with both hands...its brains or its looks"...I think we now know which category our little Brynn falls in! Lisa is just full of wisdom. Let it be said; we had a Merry Thanksgiving that year!

Everyone needs an original Halloween costume! Paul and I bought one for Beau on our own...with no child input on our vacation in early September one year. I know we both laughed like hyenas when we saw it. We said if Beau didn't like it...no problem...we would return it. But guess what...it was a HIT!!!! You are probably asking yourselves, how could a costume be so funny? What was it? I am embarrassed to say this, but it was a whoopie cushion. He ripped the plastic, and just couldn't get to it fast enough he was so thrilled with our selection for him. He puts it on at warp speed and says, "Hey Brynn, I'm going to lay down in the floor...come sit on me"...then he proceeds to make a fart noises...really nice and great etiquette.

Paul and I were so proud, as you can imagine. Oh and guess what Brynn wanted to be for Halloween the next year? Yep, a whoopie cushion! Unbeknownst to us we were raising little recyclers. Looks like, we were going green with a second use of the "tooting" costume. Minus the methane gas, of course, the EPA would be so proud.

Bedtime was quickly approaching and Paul goes into Beau's room, just to check on things. The days leading up to this night consisted of lots of stimming and "misbehaving". He enters the room to find Beau on his bed partially under his comforter but with his little rear, facing the door and Paul can see it. Paul knows at this point something fishy is going on (as Beau's favorite thing to do is hold Scoot's the cat hostage). Paul quietly creeps over to him and swats him on the butt, and just as predicted, the cat is under the covers. Beau raises his head up and tells Paul he needs his help because...and I quote, "I have a bad case of the can't stop its". Anybody aware of a program Paul and I can implement to help him with this?

One weekend in September, we had the distinct pleasure of hosting Paul's family reunion at a local park here in our community. Everyone invited attended, it was awesome!

Apparently, Beau and Brynna's branches are much closer to their third cousins on the family tree than one might have suspected. Paul's cousins have some of the cutest and funniest kids I have ever met, outside of our own, of course. His cousin Shellie has a little guy, Isaac, who at only 4 years was wise beyond his years. The kid had me in stitches. His Dad and Mom are both very witty and he exudes both of them.

In my full-time job in the cancer field, I am blessed with a wonderful program assistant, Charlotte. Charlotte is bilingual (lived in Venezuela for 14 years), as are her children. One of her daughter's, Emma, actually taught Shellie and Rick's kids Spanish. I, of course knew this, so I began a conversation with Isaac. I asked him if Ms. Emma was his Spanish teacher. He excitedly said "YES!" He loves Emma. I told her she and I were friends. Oh, that made him even happier. I asked him if he knew Spanish, again he enthusiastically said, "OH YES!" After that kind of response, I was eager to test out his Spanish skills and asked him, "Can you say 'My name is Isaac' in Spanish". He looked at me, swallowed hard, and I could see those wheels churning in his mind...I couldn't wait for that sweet little voice to speak to me in a different language. Instead, he looks at me and very seriously says, "My name is Isaac...

in Spanish". The he says, "So, how'd I do?" Hmmmm, Ms. Emma would be SO proud!

Apparently Beau has a style all of his own. So much so that his teacher, Ms. Gillim shared an incident she knew I would appreciate,

"I wanted to tell you, I just came from lunch with my kiddos. Beau eats at the same time. Ms. Ashby told me that earlier she tried to help him with his collar (it is standing up). He told her no, he wanted it "popped." She and I thought it was hilarious that he knew that."

I thought Ms. Gillim knew us better than than that. They may be teaching him about reading, writing and arithmetic but we are schooling him on looking and feeling good. I'm not surprised at all; Paul and I are sort of trailblazers in the fashion world ourselves. Our kids come by it honest. Insert uproarious belly laugh here please!

It's a Bobcat!

In Kentucky, we have quite a rivalry. Those of you, who reside here, know EXACTLY what I am talking about. It's the University of Louisville Cardinals vs. the University of Kentucky Wildcats. Now, I was raised in a home where sports were more of an afterthought than a weekly ritual or weekend event.

UK fans, this may be tough for you to read. However, I (not Paul) briefly considered the thought of naming Beau after a former UK player. Paul and I liked his character, that didn't happen but, I don't "hate" UK or any other team for that matter.

The day was my 32nd birthday and Brynna came running in the house wishing me a Happy Birthday and telling me she had made a picture for me. Before she hands it to me, she INSISTS..."I KNOW this MAY look like a Wildcat...but it's <u>NOT</u>...it's definitely a bobcat. Did you get that Mom? It's <u>NOT</u> a Wildcat. We don't like Wildcat's, it's a bobcat." Okay...GOT IT...it's a stinkin' bobcat for Pete's sake. Paul felt so esteemed she would point this out, as did I.

Later in the evening, while going through her school folder I found a 4-H interest form for kids to sign-up for the 4-H programs through the University of Kentucky Cooperative Extension Services. I faintly saw the UK logo on the top of the form. I enjoyed 4-H very much as a kid, but think Brynn's too young to appreciate it now. I put it in a pile of papers to throw away. The form happened to be on the top of the pile, she stops and takes a good look at it and VERY SERIOUSLY says, "Mom, <u>THANK YOU</u> for throwing this away, we <u>DO</u> <u>NOT</u> like UK or their programs". Oh, the laughter that ensued, there after! I guess we should work on the appropriate times to say those things, in our house she is safe. We realize is may seem as though she has been indoctrinated, and that assumption would be accurate. It's also a good possibility she could be lynched by some of those crazed UK fans. But, I think she can take them! We raise try to raise our kids right and apparently along the way they have developed a strong dislike for that "other" Kentucky team, you will have to take that up with their Father.

One of "THOSE" Houses

Do any of you have one of THOSE houses in your neighborhood...you know the one I'm talking about. You are pretty sure someone lives there because the yard is mowed... but other than that, it somewhat the phenomenon of the street. You know, it's a very nice house, mind you, it really but something is awry with it.

Well the neighborhood we visited this particular Halloween had "one of those" houses. It actually gave me the willies just to walk by it. Why? Well it's not so much that the house is creepy, per say, but more that it has so many faux flowers...animals...STUFF that just seems so un-natural outside of a home. If this is YOUR house...your grandmas, aunts, or another family member, please let me apologize in advance...and you may want to stop reading this!

It never fails, it's Halloween and the kids wanted to go to EVERY HOUSE...and yes I mean EVERY house.... including the faux everything house. Though it was against my better judgement, who am I to not allow my kids to enjoy the candy from the kind people in this neighborhood?

Beau and Brynn had a system with each home, during their trick or treating, it was alternating doorbell rings.

This house was Brynna's turn to ring the bell. Navigating through all the festivities around the front walk of this house is like an obstacle course. I thought I was going to have to GPS or Mapquest them out of there. It was touch and go for a while. I even contemplated telling them to drop their candy on the ground and use it as a means to find their way out. Brynn makes it up to the door (as I stand on the sidewalk). She's looking around...and looking around...and I'm wondering what she's doing. She's getting frustrated...and I mean REALLY frustrated. If I haven't already established this point, my kids have two volumes... LOUD and asleep. Finally, she yells, "there so much stuff up here on this porch I can't find the doorbell". I am about to DIE as other families are trick or treating and my daughter is berating the stranger's house in broad daylight. I said, "Honey, just knock on the door"...as those words leave my mouth...she yells back to me, "Never mind Mom, FOUND IT, it was behind all these vines". I am about to bury myself in their yard of junk at the embarrassment my daughter has just caused me. I suppose I should be thankful because they weren't even home. I was a bit sad because I didn't get to see the owners of "the house".

I wanted to take a picture of this house and so I did, just because I'm known for my comedic antics...some think they may think this particular incident was embellished for comedies sake but I do have a photo to prove it. However, I am sure the nice folks that live there wouldn't appreciate my story and definitely not the photo. I know it's wrong, but I am thankful for their decorations, because it more than made that Halloween memorable!

The Tree of Thanks

The night was filled with anticipation at our kids elementary school was going to have a pajama party night. Brynn was ecstatic beyond words as she talked about it for at least 2 weeks. I promised to take her and was actually looking forward to it myself; however I didn't think the whole school would want to see me in yoga pants and a t-shirt from circa 2000, so I wore my work clothes...OOPS digression...back to Brynn. I broke out some iCarly pajamas we bought for her for Christmas (ummmm, I mean Santa) for this special occasion. Beau just wasn't interested in going BACK to school after a day of hard work (insert Mommy's infamous eye roll here!).

Tuesday evening at 5:30, we arrived at the school. The parking lot and school entrance was filled little pajama clad cuties everywhere! Brynn and I walk in to have our picture made then proceed to the library where the "formal" part of the evening was to begin. We make our way to an empty table and find a seat. The first portion was adorable as Brynna's teacher from kindergarten played the part of Amelia Bedilia and acted out part of a story. Next was reading with your child. Brynn was reading too me and it really blessed my heart. She's a great little reader and I enjoyed it immensely.

Next, she was able to take a test over the book she had just read to me and it would count toward the accelerated reader program. I was super excited for her when she got a 100%! This night wasn't just fun, but also useful for her! I love this school, apart from my earlier puns, they know they are apart of our stories!

Now this is where things started to go downhill...I'm not sure, if it was an intentional plot against the parents or if it was just my child. Now it's craft time...woo-hoo...who doesn't love a good craft, right?! I already told you, I am absolutely terrible at anything artistic but I swallowed my pride and would do it for my girl on pajama night. Each parent and child was given a "kit" to make a picture frame that called a Tree of Thanks. The photo taken when we entered the building was to go in the frame. I look all around at all the frames lying on the table. Kids were encouraged to write things they are thankful for on the leaves. I can see many leaves that say, "Mommy, Mom, Momma" this was going on this thankful tree. They were thankful for their Mommies. But also, as I looked around, I could see many other things listed that the kids were thankful for, but I can't wait for Brynn to put my name down on her tree. I'll tell you Brynn's ended up looking like. Well my girl starts off slow, and she says "Leaves, I'm thankful for leaves"... so we write it...she then proceeds to give me a myriad of answers, "Daddy"..."Bubby"..."Job"..."Scoots" (yes our two cats 'made the tree' of thanks!)..."Memaw"..."Papaw"...."C hloe"...."Aunt Nay Nay"….Nana….Granny..."Mamaw"... and she named several others...but we ran out of leaves (so DON'T be offended!!!).

Anyone missing...I mean anyone OBVIOUS missing? Yep...that's right...I didn't make the "Tree of Thanks"! The one, who threw up almost every day in her office trash, carried her in her womb for 9 months and who endured a birth with NO epidural (cause it didn't take!)...who has loved her unconditionally (at least up to this point). Yep, if I were you and you didn't make the "Tree" I would NOT be offended. But, if you were ME, I bet YOU would!

I wish I could say it ended there, we kissed and made up and that was that, but the saga continued...as did the downward spiral. Now as the pajama party winds down, it was time to go the final activity of this ONCE fun evening. It's the cornucopia snack mix...a fellow mother joked..."Maybe there will be a turkey leg in there"...no chance...cheerios, cheese balls, peanuts (maybe), raisins, M&Ms and pretzels (a feast fit for a pilgrim). Anyway, it looked appetizing. However, they were running low and I didn't take a portion... actually, I just knocked a kindergartner down and grabbed hers. KIDDING!

It was at this time that Brynn decided once and for all to finish me off...she stuck a dagger in my already weak heart. She looks at me, with cornucopia in hand and says, "Mom, you're not going to sit by me are you?"...I said "yes, I planned on it". She said, "Please don't, I want you to sit "OVER THERE". My mouth flung open in disbelief...remember I am a really cool Mom. I am then relegated, by my first grader, to a table next to "her table"...I could have fought it, but my heart was already in disarray after not making the Tree of Thanks...so I just sat there and felt sorry for myself and was writing this story in my head already.

I had been texting Paul through out the evening, giving him the 411 on pajama night activities. He texted back after the Tree of Thanks..."LOL". As I walked in the door, I told him..."Hey, it's not funny, you had a leaf on the tree and I didn't". What an insensitive reaction he gave...LOL. You just wait until she breaks your heart I told him, its coming, buddy!

As the evening comes to a painful close, I asked Brynn why she didn't put me on her tree. She said, "I am thankful for you Mom"...as she looks down at her bare feet. I said why didn't you put me on there then (obviously still reeling from the rejection). She shrugs her shoulders...thinks a minute... and then says with a pleased smile..."I'm thankful for you the MOST...you get your OWN tree"!!!!! Did you hear that Memaw, Daddy, Papaw...and all you other people and things that made the tree...I get MY OWN TREE!

I hugged her...whispered in her ear "Good answer baby!"...and sent her off to bed. If you think for one minute I think I am the one she is most thankful for, I have some ocean front property in Arizona I'd like to sell you...right next to George Straight and his property!

All seemed well until the next night. I see my sweet little Brynn perched on the bar in our kitchen with a magic marker. What does she have in front of her? None other than her "tree of thanks" picture frame. I look down and can see she has written my name on the frame and marked my Mom's name out. I smile and say, "Honey, you didn't have to mark Memaw's name out, I didn't mind". She said, "I know, I put your name on there because I've decided to give Memaw her OWN tree". GROAN!!!!!!!! It was at that point I considered rewriting our entire will and just leaving everything to Beau. Ha ha ha!

Breathe Right

As you have already witnessed through this book... RANDOM things happen to me. I'm not sure if Murphy's Law should be called Jaime's Law...cause if it can happen; I seem to be the one it happens too. Let's recap...just for fun! Two car accidents in a matter of months, falling in an open parking lot at Target with HOT coffee in my hands, a stranger whacking me on the backside in broad day light at Books-A-Million because he had me mistaken for someone else. This morning is NO different. However, it's not to the magnitude of the others. I just feel like God wants me to laugh at life...specifically...my own!

Okay, so this morning I get up. Go to the mirror and notice my hair is matted at the bottom left corner. So I begin to run my hand through it...the hand gets stuck. I am wondering if a small bird has nested in my head overnight... and I am unaware of it. I mean this is a feat, and I'm afraid I'm going to have to call in for back up (all I had at my disposal were two cats and two kids...it was looking like dire straights here). Whatever it is doesn't seem to want to budge. I just pray I don't have to "cut" it out!!! I know I didn't go to bed with gum in my mouth!

Anyway, I FINALLY (3-minute lapse here) get my hand through it. I then am able to pull my hand away to see what is stuck to my finger. Low and behold, Paul's Breathe Right Nasal strip is STUCK in it. I mean what did I plow my head right on his face in the middle of the night or what??? This is weird too me. Did he even wonder where it went? If yes, I have the answer! Think about it...how well could he REALLY be breathing last night? I am not sure how long he had no nasal strip, and from the looks of it, he had a mass of dark auburn hair over his face. That could not have produced a good mood.

This evening I am trying to conjure a way from this happening again...I am open to ideas. A.) Buzz cut hair B.) Wrap it in a turban style towel wrap (girl's you know the one) C.) Duct Tape the Breathe Right Strip to Paul's face (then run the risk of getting Duct Tape in my hair next...NICE!).

You can see I am not very good at trouble-shooting. I did share this unfortunate incident with a few of my friends. I couldn't believe some of the stories they had on the strips. When placed properly on your nose, they are wonderful. Like your nasal passages open immediately. But, when put on your eyebrow, they can also act as a hair removal system, one friend told me. The problem was she didn't need an eyebrow wax that day. I will just chalk this one up for me as another Rafferty mishap. By the way, I can't tell if it's just me or if this random event has allowed my hair to breathe better. Perhaps through no effort of my own, and unbeknownst to Paul, we have created a new hair care treatment. I will absolutely have to share this with my stylist Tonya. Who knows, the nasal strip company may have just found a new market.

Wash Your Hands

I am not sure, if the region of the US you are in has been inundated with talk of the swine flu over the last couple of years, but here in our "neck of the woods" the talk was big. Rightfully so, of course. I am in the public health field and really appreciate the media alerts and messaging about the importance of practical ways to help avoid the flu.

At one point in my career, I actually worked for our district health department. I loved working for our state public health system. I have become a sucker for epidemiology (prior to my employment there I thought this was a layer of skin), environmental services and vaccination schedules. I often joked with my colleagues that they had hired the wrong girl. I was a bit of an alarmist. If you said, "Anthrax", I would be like "What??? Evacuate the building". Mind you, you could have been talking about germ warfare in general, and I was certain the mention of the word meant it was in my vicinity. However, time spent there was a welcomed education for me and I am a huge advocate of public health for it. So now, for this reason, bird flu, swine flu and any other flu, though very serious doesn't scare me much anymore.

I was able to use some of my public health knowledge with my little scholars on the way to school one morning. I decided to talk to them about the flu bug. Beau had been repeatedly asking, "What's a flu bug". I told him "icky germs that make people sick". I reiterated hand washing, coughing into your elbow (should you need to cough) and keeping our hands to ourselves. No sooner than the words left my mouth Brynna says, "Mom, I know, I know Blake (a fellow kindergartner) told me <u>all</u> about the importance of hand washing and the flu yesterday!" Maybe Blake should send his resume to the district health department, he's already got a leg up on me it looks like, I was at least in my mid-twenties by the time I had all that information.

So in flu season and beyond, DON'T forget to wash your hands...this message is brought to you by Blake (and his sweet mommy Jennifer! Blake WAS listening, Jennifer.).

MINE!

I told you earlier, I really love Proverbs 31 and for good reason...it tells me I can LAUGH at the days to come. Laughs just seem to abound at the Rafferty house. In this spirit, I will share how our well-behaved children (insert HARD SWALLOW) handled a situation one evening.

For whatever reason I was exhausted on this given night. I had planned to fix a "real" supper (this means not from the freezer or pantry), but couldn't bring myself to do it. I had some frozen ravioli and a jar alfredo sauce. That was supper... oh and some frozen garlic bread. The kids seem to be under the impression that this is "grown-up" food. Paul and I don't make them eat this particular supper. I suppose that's another strike against me in the running for Mother of the Year. That evening the kids had a "Holy" supper. Growing up my Mom called it "seek and ye shall find". This was the rummaging in the Rafferty fridge and cupboards. Brynn knew exactly what she wanted!! YAY! That was awesome for me because she is my "ponderer". You can seriously give her NO MORE than one option...you would be there all night, because like many of us women...she can never make up her mind. Then it was sweet Beau's turn to select his supper. Though a bit particular he knows exactly what he wants, when he wants it. And that night, what did he want? A can of "Brynna's" soup.

Now, I am not sure why it is that kids feel like items in the house our theirs. To my knowledge neither one of our children have financially contributed to our household! And if they have...where's the beef??? Anyway, I think we as parents, unfortunately, contribute to this by says..."that's Brynna's...that's Beau's".

SO...here we are. Beau wants "Brynna's" Mega-Noodle Campbell's soup. Brynn takes one look at the can and is some how able to put her bottom lip in a stance in which I have never seen before...it reminded me of a fork-lift... moving up and down as this conversation progressed. Quite a phenomenon, if you ask me! She just yells, "MINE!" Instead of taking the darn can and fixing it because Paul and I paid for it with our hard-earned money...I become immersed in a battle of the wits with my 6 year-old. I KNOW BETTER!!! Paul is smart...he is not in the room, and doesn't want to be a part of it. Beau is standing there...looking famished... possibly wanting me to knock his sister into next week. Again, she yells, "MINE!"

In true super hero fashion...I say, "Beau, you know what? You can have this soup". VICTORY IS MINE, I have now reclaimed my role as PARENT! I then do what every child hates...especially stubborn little Brynna. It's cruel and unusual punishment...but I like it...I make them hug one another. Beau is ready for the hug, he loves his little sister and he has just gotten "his way"...it's good to be Beau in the situation. So, they embrace. Brynna's bottom lip is still on the kitchen floor. I tell them to say, "I love you"...yes, I know...I am taking it a bit too far...why?? BECAUSE I CAN! Brynn wraps her little arms around Beau and mumbles what sounds like, "I bub oohh"...But I knew what it was...

close enough. Beau goes in for the hug...smiles as big as the morning sun and says, ***"Brynna, I love you too, but I don't like*** <u>that</u> ***attitude right now"***. OH, BEAU...that was GREAT!

So, when it looks like all hope is lost and you have failed as a parent...force them to hug and I bet one of those rotten little blessings will take the words right out of your mouth!!

Believe it or not, this book is divinely inspired. You might be questioning that some of the stories are from the Lord. Though I know through scripture, I am "fearfully and wonderfully made", I am also a flawed human like you, so these stories are a little "irregular" at times as well. Just look at them like they are from God's Outlet Mall. I feel humbled that he allowed the Rafferty's to live them and laugh at them. Because of this, we know that God wants to us to appreciate the things he has given us in life, even the funny things.

I often have to search for peace. I worry like a Grandma. I think I will make an awesome Grandma someday because I already have the worrywart mentality of most sweet little Grannies. The was probable the only quality that I didn't want to inherit from my precious Mammaw Evelyn, and what happened...it was the one I got... the worry gene (yes, I think it's our genetic make-up...this isn't a scientific fact more of a my own perception but I do have a college degree). I take that back, I got a couple of others...I still think the Golden Girls are hysterical...as she did...and I absolutely love to shop. Mammaw, thank you for those last two, I really appreciate them. Unfortunately, that worry gene has wasted many days of my life. God has given me a formula to help me overcome it, if I just rest on his word.

I am reminded that peace and joy are available to me and all other believers because of Jesus Christ. I especially love Romans chapter 5.

Romans 5:1-11 (New International Version)

Peace and Joy

[1]Therefore, since we have been justified through faith, we have peace with God through our Lord Jesus Christ, [2]through whom we have gained access by faith into this grace in which we now stand. And we rejoice in the hope of the glory of God. [3]Not only so, but we also rejoice in our sufferings, because we know that suffering produces perseverance; [4]perseverance, character; and character, hope. [5]And hope does not disappoint us, because God has poured out his love into our hearts by the Holy Spirit, whom he has given us. [6]You see, at just the right time, when we were still powerless, Christ died for the ungodly. [7]Very rarely will anyone die for a righteous man, though for a good man someone might possibly dare to die. [8]But God demonstrates his own love for us in this: While we were still sinners, Christ died for us. [9]Since we have now been justified by his blood, how much more shall we be saved from God's wrath through him! [10]For if, when we were God's enemies, we were reconciled to him through the death of his Son, how much more, having been reconciled, shall we be saved through his life! [11]Not only is this so, but we also rejoice in God through our Lord Jesus Christ, through whom we have now received reconciliation.

I will admit, much of my suffering has been needlessly, pretty much self-imposed. By this I mean, I have made some bone-headed decisions that were out of the will of God and I have suffered because of it, and worse than that is that, I have caused others to suffer because of my own lackluster decisions. That is NOT good! However as verse three reminds us, so much does come out of suffering whether it be at our own hand or at the hands of another. I tell you what; I think I probably have enough character to go around for us all. I have built so much character in my day, and I am only in my 30's. I really don't see the construction of my character coming to an end, anytime soon. I'm reminded as I continue reading that through God sending his Son to die for me and thankfully, I have received reconciliation for those bonehead mistakes. Now, that doesn't give me a license to go out and be a bonehead all over again. But, more over, I can rejoice that I as a lost sheep, have been found and the penalty for my mistakes, has been paid in full. God is my bondsmen. I am responsible to him for an account of things to come. But the slate is wiped clean and I'm not on parole. Whew, that legal jargon was starting to frighten me.

I can't help myself...stop reading if you want. I won't be offended. These stories are most likely more of a gift to me, as to those who are reading them. I know they are from God as he has allowed me to collect our memories. He designed me with the purpose of encouraging others. I can't think of a better way to accomplish this than through a little more laughter. I just love to laugh (in case that point has been driven home enough through these stories)...please laugh with me...there is still more.

Snow White and Seven Reindeer... What?

There's nothing like a little Christmas cheer...I mean I like it as much as the next guy/gal right? Well one December evening, Brynn and I had the awesome privilege of seeing the musical The Wizard of Oz at our community's beautiful performing arts center, compliments of my dear friend, Karen. The only thing missing from this GRAND performance was Paul and Beau!

I have to be honest...sorry Karen...it was touch and go for a while. Here we got these great tickets, to a sold out performance for free and Brynn was scared out of her ever-loving head at times. She asked me several times if we could just leave. I hate to say it, but I contemplated it because her fright became my misery! I was glad that she had decided by intermission, just to spite the witch, she was going to stay to watch her melt. (TAKE THAT!) Or at least that's what she told me.

Back to the Christmas cheer...during intermission, Brynna decides it would be a good time to do a review of all of Santa's reindeer. I was good with that, it passed the time and it forced me to see if I could recall them all. We begin...not in order of the classic song Rudolph the Red Nose Reindeer. More in MY order...which is a bit hodge-podgey. I begin, "There's Donner, Blitzen, Rudolph, Comet, Cupid, Dancer, Prancer" (I'm not even really sure if I am naming them correctly, but Brynn seems to be going right along with me.) So we sit there, with people all around us, just waiting for the next act and she says, "Mom that's not all of them". We review again...this time Brynn using her fingers to count each reindeer I list. At this point, I am a little tired of the game....and feel like it would be the perfect time to interject a little holiday cheer of my own. I then review the names again, after Prancer; I very nonchalantly say Sleepy, Dopey and Sneezy. She lifts a finger for each name I call...not getting it. She looks at me and counts again and says, aloud..."Sleepy, Dopey and Sneezy"...still counting. Then, a light bulb goes off and she says, "MOM, those aren't Santa's reindeer they are the Dwarfs!" We have our own little audience in the Mezzanine that erupted in laughter. Bet they didn't realize they were getting two shows for the price of one!

Next time your in a jam and can't name all the reindeer, just interject some Dwarfs...its all good...I won't judge you... PROMISE! Just don't do it in front of Brynna...she's a sharp one...after she reviews them in her head and on her fingers a time or two!

Wherever You Go...There You Are!

Have you ever arrived somewhere (i.e. work, church, and home) and wondered how in the world did you get there? That is me many mornings. One morning, I arrived at work and was like WHOA (that was inspire by Joey from Blossom for those of you who grew up in the same era as me!)...surely I haven't been driving...cause I have NO clue how I got here...really safe stuff!

I dreamed non-stop that night before, maybe that's why I was so tired. From what I remembered...my friend that was in the "Shovette" when it supposedly backfired, Jill, was playing a supporting role in this dream. I was riding a unicycle down the highway, and happened to see my friend Jill not on a unicycle, but in a street legal vehicle. I had actually been to her house (apparently it was unlocked) and I ran in and stole a bunch of carnival tickets and was going to cash them in for prizes. The problem was...she passed me on the highway... and I on the unicycle was holding this mountain of tickets...while maneuvering the unicycle. I never knew I had such an ability to multitask. It's no wonder I was so sleepy...I was busy. I am so glad I cannot see inside my own mind, it would scare the living daylights out of me.

I have never had any desire to ride a unicycle, or use it as a get-away vehicle after I have stolen carnival tickets from a dear friend. Perhaps my children are more like me than I want to validate.

It was a Friday afternoon and I picked the kids up from school. As I am driving some how Brynn gets on the subject of the Bible. I love it, and am excited. Paul and I have really been in the word and studying it for ourselves. I was hoping that whatever biblical question she sent my way, I could actually answer it. Anyway, she starts asking me how could David have been a king when God is the king. I try to explain David was the king of a land and God is the king of everything (how'd I do people out there with older kiddos?). She then begins to ask about Jesus. I tell her that Jesus is God in the flesh...so she is trying to ask if he is King. I emphatically tell her YES. She says, "Wait a minute...I thought Jesus was God's son". Oh here we go! I go into the whole, "God in the flesh...God in skin" explanation, quickly realizing, much like the thunder and lightening event when she was in daycare, even I am confusing myself. She then says with a sigh..."Well I just think Jesus is God's assistant! Everybody knows he sits at the right hand of God. All assistants sit at the right hand of their boss." Ok Brynn...you may have just re-written the bible with the whole assistant analogy but you are very close with your explanation. From now on, I think Paul and I are just going to have standing appointments with our pastor, Brother James for Brynna.

We will continue to educate ourselves every day and through bible study on Sunday. The following Sunday, we leave in PLENTY of time for church. We are on the bypass around the city and Paul realizes he's forgotten his cell phone. He is on call at work that weekend so he has to have it. We just make a big circle (NO U-TURNS though). We exited the by-pass, just to get right back on to head home.

This took maybe 2 -3 minutes, at most. We stopped at a stop light and Brynn says, "I thought we were going to church". Paul and I both said simultaneously, "We are". She said with the most serious tone, "Why did we go ALL (we went about a MILE) that way just to end up here?" (at a stoplight about a mile from our house). We both busted out laughing...Brynn and Beau both say, "What's so funny, why we are going back home...we didn't even go to church". We didn't really need Paul's cell phone. We just thought it might be fun just to confuse the children.

I wanted to tell Brynn...you have NO idea how many times in your life you will feel like you have been around the world either figuratively or literally just to end back up in the same place you started...can I get an Amen?!

So in the immortal words of Clint Black..."Wherever you go...there you are"...thanks Clint...I couldn't have figured that one out by myself. Wherever I go...there, I am...DUH!

Pile Me Up!

Beau has this habit of sneaking into our room and just planting himself at the end of our bed. Either we are too lazy to have him go back in his room at times, or it goes unnoticed until the alarm wakes us up. One morning Beau popped in the bed about 5am. I think the anticipation of his class Christmas party that day was just too much for him.

As he and Brynn sat in our bed while I am getting ready, they are watching Blue's Clues on Nick Jr. Blue is giving clues to her favorite part of school. Beau decides he's going to play his own game. So he says, "Hey Brynny, wanna guess what my favorite part of school is?" Silence! "Hey Brynny, I said, wanna guess what my favorite part of school is?" Again, silence! Finally with a little more assertion Beau literally clears his throat and says, "Brynny, I SAID, wanna guess what my favorite part of school is?" She looks at him, smiles her toothless grin and says, "I don't know, science?" He says, "No way, it LUNCH of course!" Perhaps I should be dining at the elementary school "Cafe" if it's that good Ms. Donna! Do you all deliver?

That same morning we are all ready to leave. There is a pile...yes I said a pile...of presents by the garage door. I had

Beau a stack for his teachers and Brynn a stack for hers. We LOVE our school and I love the staff. Beau takes one look a the "stack" and says, "I am NOT carrying all those". He is dead set on just taking only the gift for "Derrick" the boy's name he drew for the class party. Mind you, he had about 3 other presents to disseminate that day, but he was having NO part of it. I coaxed him into putting them into a bag and then carrying his "main" teacher's gift (which was in a larger gift bag). He acted as if I had just asked him to donate one of his kidneys. A real scene...if you will!

Then, Brynn is the opposite and says, "Pile me up, I can carry them ALL". Hmmm...don't know how many of you have seen her in "real" life. She's not bigger than a minute and comes up to my kneecap...in heels (kidding of course!). She has on her winter coat, which is bigger than she is, and has a slew of presents in her sweet little arms. I can tell she's getting top heavy...swaying side to side. I quickly realize that was not going to work, and I say, "Let's rethink this". She said, "Yeah I never carried presents and walked at that same time". That was pretty obvious...she has the grace of her Mother, so I had a back-up plan. I put one of gifts in the backpack (goodness only knows what it ended up looking like...but it was for Coach Al, and no offense but men are SO much less judgmental when it comes to the appearance of things...I thought Coach Al could care less if it looked it has been slept on!). At that point, we are ready to leave the house.

The car ended up being a whole different feat. Let's just say it was a tight squeeze in the back seat according to the two elves I was transporting. We pull up to school and I give them the go ahead to unbuckle. They literally are slowly pouring out of the car with all the stuff their Momma has packed for them. As they get out...it is reminiscent of Randy...Ralphie's little brother on a Christmas story. The mother bundles him up and then he falls on the sidewalk and can't get up. I played this scenario over in my head... Beau or Brynna falling (not hurting themselves of course) with all these presents and not being able to get up. People looking as if they are rushing to their aid only to confiscate the presents and leaving my two sweeties their to fend for themselves (okay so I am a little dramatic, but that's what I thought!!!) But luckily, they waddled in the school with no event! WHEW...talk about a close call!

I'm hoping social services won't be called in over this incident after the school personnel got a good look at them and all their "stuff" that day. I can just see Paul and I, being charged with cruel and unusual punishment of a minor (they looked like jet-puffed marshmallows fighting for air!)... hopefully after they saw some of their gifts they realized the cruel and unusual treatment wasn't in vain, it really was all for them!

I Need a Bumpit

The Christmas holiday season recently passed. I was reflecting on it; this Christmas season specifically. I'm a person who doesn't mind to receive presents, of course, it's always nice, but I really enjoy giving the gifts. I was thinking about just how giving Santa was this year and if Dave Ramsey would approve of his shopping/spending habits. I was thinking, did we put the emphasis where it needed it to be…on Jesus Christ? I'm reminded that we really tried too, yes. Paul and I would ask the kids each night during winter break what Christmas meant and they would tell us Jesus' birthday. We will build upon this each year, as they mature and really begin to appreciate His birth.

I also had some silly observations. Take this for example; did I really NEED a Bumpit? No, not really. If you don't know what a Bumpit is, where have you been? The Bumpit is a real phenomenon. It consists of a hard piece of plastic that comes in a variety of colors to match the majority of basic hair colors. Its purpose is to give the hair that extra lift around your crown. I can't believe I just referenced that a Bumpit has a true purpose. Since I can do that, if you are looking for your "purpose" in life, just holler at me, if I can find a purpose for a hair accessory, finding one for a person should be no challenge at all.

I'm normally not a sucker for infomercial goodies… unlike my husband and daughter, as you have learned. However, I was completely captivated by the Bumpit. I mean, what woman doesn't want her hair to have body and lift? This is a completely rhetorical question…especially for those reading this, shaking your head thinking, "No way, I don't want or need that". For some oddball reason, I thought I "needed" one. The funny thing is, I walked by them a million times at our local super center and also never picked up the phone at the sight of the infomercial. It was just one of those things in the back of your head telling you, "you should get one of those". It wasn't God; luckily I could differentiate his will from my want. So, I wanted one. Like any other Southern beauty…and beauty wannabe, I let my Momma buy me a Bumpit for Christmas. It's one of those items I wanted but didn't want to splurge on for myself. I really allowed my Mom to splurge at $9.99 a pop, huh? That's another thing, how funny is it that thought of this hairpiece as a splurge. I seem to be going further into the Twilight Zone here, don't I?

Anyway, my curious mind was too much for me to pass up using the Bumpit almost immediately. I received it on Christmas Eve at Mom and Dad's in the early afternoon. By 4:00pm that day I had the box ripped open and I was eager to use it so I could be "bumped" for our next family gathering with Paul's family. I'm standing in my bathroom; not reading the directions, which I suppose would have been more helpful, trying to insert this unique hair device. My daughter is mumbling something behind me; again I remind you she's six at this time. I am almost positive she is trying to instruct me how to insert the Bumpit. I turn around look at her and ask her what she's saying. She says very seriously, "I'm trying to tell you how to put in your Bumpit". I am almost dumbfounded and am now thinking of calling the Bumpit company to advertise, "So easy a 6 year old could do it", but then I'd have to fess up that I am making a mockery of this great invention. She then walks me through, step-by-step, what sections of my hair to raise, tease, then place the device on and gently press down. So, I do exactly what she says. I look in the mirror and begin laughing at myself uncontrollably. I think I actually began breaking a sweat trying to get my hair to lie perfectly. Now, I have to be honest, I did not wear it that evening. I was just too stressed to get it exactly how I wanted it. However, I haven't given up on the Bumpit completely. I'm thinking when I have a good 3-4 hours to devote too it, I should be fine. You know what they say, "Slow and steady wins the race".

Growing Pains

For some reason, I'm sure at one point it was a good reason. My husband and I thought that Brynna needed to refrain from drinking coffee. The verbiage used when telling her may have been along the lines of, "it will stunt your growth"...which we translated to her, "you won't grow if you drink it". Now, if you told me to refrain from it, I might have a bit of temper tantrum, but now that I think I am done growing, we are all safe. Coffee is my guilty pleasure. I could drink it (and usually do) from sun-up to sundown on days that end in Y. In all seriousness, if I recall correctly, we initially didn't want her to have the coffee was more about her thinking she was older than she and coffee is usually what adults drink. We probably should give her at least a gallon a day because as it is she's growing to fast and I would like for her to stop...but I guess that's not God's will either, huh?

Back to the coffee. On this particular occasion, Brynn sheepishly approaches me as I am getting ready for work on a Monday morning. I feel her tug on my pants as I am putting the finishing touches on "the look" for the day. I turn around to see my sweet girl somewhat bewildered. I am thinking to myself, "Now what's wrong?" Over that weekend she had stayed with my parents. Side note here, my kids adore their Grandparents…all of them. Brynn had stayed two nights with them, while Beau was only up for one night. Anyway, Brynna looks up at me with those big blue eyes and says, "Memaw MIGHT have let me have coffee". I said, "Okay, you know what your Daddy and I say about this right?" With tears in her eyes she looks at me and says, "My legs are hurting, that's a good sign". I said, "What are you talking about, your legs hurting?" She said, "Well once you told me those are growing pains, and my legs are hurting, so the coffee must not have stopped my growth, I think I'm growing right now".

Guess she showed me the old coffee would stunt your growth trick is just an evil ploy used by parents and grandparents alike to save all the coffee for ourselves. I wouldn't be surprised if the next time we go out for breakfast if she asks the waitress for a cup of coffee. What's next, will she want it black? If yes, I know she's growing up way too fast!

King?

It was my first day back to work since December 18. I wasn't ready or willing but duty calls and the money is good.

I have to admit I thought I wanted to come back to work, because I am woman called into the work force... or so I thought...until I saw my kids that first afternoon after being off with them for just over two weeks. I missed them like crazy! We had a WONDERFUL Christmas break together.

During those long breaks Paul and I let the kids sleep in Beau's bed. They are sometimes like twins...attached at the hip. Almost immediately upon getting in our car that first afternoon back in the routine Brynn asks if she can sleep in Beau's bed January 17th, because school is out January 18th. I told her, "Sure".

She then begins to tell me its Martin Luther King Day and there is no school. She continues by saying that it must be important to be out of school. She then asks me who he is and I begin to tell her...in true fashion, there I go again giving too deep of an explanation (OH WELL! You live, you learn.). She says, "I don't understand what you just said, but Mrs. Daugherty said it was his birthday". I just smile and say, "Oh yeah, that's right". Wishing she would have saved me ALL that trouble. She then says, "Was he a King?" (I'm reminded of the Jesus and David conversation and I begin to dread where this is going) I said, "No, King was his last name". She said, "No it isn't!" I said, "Yes it is, Martin Luther King (Jr.)". She said, "Uh no Mom it's not... it's Martin Luther King Day...his last name is Day".

I begin laughing like crazy, as I normally do and I tell her, "No honey that's because the DAY is in his honor, his name was Martin Luther King". She smiled and said, "Well, I wondered why he had SO MANY names". I couldn't wait to tell Paul…and you either!

I hope, if you were confused about Mr. King, that you now have your "story" straight too...if not, I hear he's not to hard to find on the web.

The Right Piece

I have an on-going and growing relationship with God. This last year has been frightening and enlightening all at once. I rest on his grace and mercy. Sharing our family with you scared me beyond words. Rejection is not one of my strong suits; in fact I was even scared to tell people God inspired me to share how he is working in my life now to make me the woman he designed me to be. He has inspired me through scripture, and calmed my fears by reminding me, it's not all about me. My relationship with Him is all about me…and him…but this life…it has so little to do with me, that isn't even funny.

He called me to search His word and look for scripture that would ease my fears and help me focus on Him, while using the skills He's given me to deal with life…like laughter! I read, believe and hope even if you are reading these particular scriptures for the hundredth time that it impacts you like it still does me.

Jeremiah 29:11 (New International Version)

[11] For I know the plans I have for you," declares the LORD, "plans to prosper you and not to harm you, plans to give you hope and a future.

Proverbs 3:5-6 (New International Version)

[5] Trust in the LORD with all your heart and lean not on your own understanding; [6] in all your ways acknowledge him, and he will make your paths straight. [a]

Maybe one of these days I will finally STOP leaning on my own understanding, which is often really faulty, and live what I am reading.

He uses my amazing husband, my precious children, my priceless family, my special friends and the wisdom of my pastors to spurn new thoughts and ideas that are not of me. I jotted down some of our life on these pages, not realizing when I began that our lives would be any more than something fun to keep and reflect on as my kids grew up and as Paul and I "grew up" too. For me, this is nothing short of an amazing spiritual journey. As I have shared these stories with you my mind and heart often felt like a fuse was about to blow and I didn't even have my hair dryer or flatiron plugged in! God was really speaking to me through this scripture, telling me through him and through a saving relationship with Jesus Christ and reminding me that "I'm not who I was", and wanted me to tell you, you don't have to be either!

See, I told you life was funny, or at least I have been blessed to see the humor in mine. Do you feel better just laughing with us? I hope so! That's what God desires for us, joyful hearts. I see God's hand in everything now, even those little things that happen around the house or the office, even in my car. Let me rephrase that, some days I have to choose to see God's hand and not forget how funny some things are. I pray the same thing for you. Think about sharing your joy with others. We often have no problem filling up a prayer list, but we should hope that God hears our praises as well.

I know it may seem elementary to some, but my prayer is that you will choose to laugh this day. Let's pray right now!

Dear Heavenly Father,

Thank you for giving us so many things in our lives to bring us joy. Please lead and guide us to choose joy, even when our circumstances would lead us to choose otherwise. We praise you for loving us enough to give us gifts that we may use to help draw others closer to you, especially laughter.

In Jesus Name, AMEN!

I hope you choose to serve the Lord in love and laughter! May you forever give God the thanks and glory for the ability to laugh even when at that moment your life may seem anything but funny. I pray you will find peace in your circumstances and search the joy that is just waiting to be uncovered in your life. Challenge yourself to find God in all things, though he often naturally reveals his hand, we must take off our rose-colored glasses tainted by the vision of the world, in order to find it. Search His word; there are so many amazing scriptures that can help you on your quest for finding peace.

Thank you for going on this journey with us. I know our story does not end here and I pray there more funny things are to come. Think about your story, and the ways God has blessed you and your family. I challenge you to write them down, or take a picture. Keep those memories close and on those days when you are feeling you don't have much to smile about, take them out and reflect upon them.

Now get out there and start living the life you were created to live and work to rediscover or find that piece that's been missing in your life. I definitely had a God shaped hole that's now made whole with Jesus. If you haven't already found that piece, Jesus is waiting and anticipating to be the Lord of your life. When I allowed Him to fill that space of the missing piece, He has lovingly given me the peace I have longed for. So, to make a long story, short, in finding the right piece, I found the right peace, His peace!

LaVergne, TN USA
20 April 2010

179769LV00001B/2/P